I'll be Glad when I've Had Enough!

To Richard.

How are [you] managing our float
and are *Right-Launcher* !!

With my very Best Wishes -

Robin Mitchell-Ball

I'll be Glad when I've Had Enough!

by

Robin Marshall-Ball

Rookmarsh Books

Published by:
Rookmarsh Books
43 Castle View
Westbury
Wiltshire BA13 3HR
www.rookmarsh.co.uk

All photographs by the author except
 p 157 and p 159 by John Dryden
Cover photo by Pam Marshall-Ball

ISBN 978-0-9561508-0-6

Also by the author

The Sporting Shotgun, A user's handbook
Saiga Books 1981
Second edition published by Swan Hill 2003

The Sporting Rifle, A user's handbook Pelham 1986
Second edition 1989
Third edition Swan Hill 1995
Fourth edition 2000
Fifth edition 2009

The Encyclopaedia of Sporting Shooting Batsford 1991

I'll be Back in an Hour! Rookmarsh Books 2007

Contents

FOREWORD

True wildfowling can only take place below the high water mark of ordinary spring tides, anything else is merely inland duck or goose shooting. Having said that, the remaining salt marshes around our coast and estuaries extend from the bare mudflats and spartina beds to the permanent salt pasture on the seaward side of the sea wall, grazing marsh dotted with the samphire, sea purslane and sea lavender. These places are truly Britain's last wildernesses.

At times they are tranquil, beautiful places were one can relax and forget life's problems, at others we see them in all their wild elemental glory, a raging torrent of storm-tossed water, driving wind, and stinging rain pushing you to the limits of endurance, with the incoming tide always eager to cut you off from the safety of the sea wall. When returning to your vehicle after such an experience you ask yourself the question "Did I really enjoy that?".

Sitting down in the warmth of your base an hour or two later, with a full stomach and a hot drink in your hand, the answer will always be "Yes.!". Nothing can compare with the experience you have just been through, of being chased off the marsh by the incoming tide, and trying to outwit the duck and geese flighting into a gale searching for a more sheltered and safe place to rest or feed.

What kind of a person gets up in the early hours when a howling gale is forecast, praying that the forecast is correct? You drive to the coast and walk two or three miles in the pre-dawn dark along the sea wall before striking out for your chosen place on the marsh. You slither into a wet draughty creek and try to keep warm while waiting for the slow winter's dawn to come, and all the time hoping that your knowledge, and the knowledge of your mentors, has got you in the right place. To shiver with cold, and then with excitement and anticipation as the faint whistles of a wigeon pack or the music of wild geese cuts through roar of wind and distant surf. Suddenly, the birds appear out of the dawn murk. Forget about wind, mud, and the cold, as birds come into range. The sense of elation as you see a cleanly killed bird topple from the sky and you immediately send the dog on its mission. When you hold your prize in your hand and praise the dog for a good retrieve, you take a quick hot drink from your thermos flask and get back to straining ears and eyes in the icy dawn light.

Such persons can truly call themselves 'Wildfowlers'

.

When I first met Robin it was obvious from the start that we were two of a kind. Though already an experienced 'fowler he was a newcomer to the Wash, and as all responsible 'fowlers do, he sought local knowledge and guidance. He never questioned the advice I offered and just did as I told him, as if I was a trusted friend of many years. It was as if we had met before, or perhaps there was that instinctive and natural bond of one true wildfowler recognizing another. Some time later, when I took up the task of helping him get his first Wash goose, I did not realize what a challenge I had set myself! And so a friendship was forged during the bitter east coast dawns.

I have a favourite remark of frustration following an unsuccessful sortie, and in Shep White's car park at Holbeach one morning the joke came back at me. "That phrase would make a good title for a Wildfowling book!"

The rest is history.

The skill of the wildfowling is still alive and being handed on. This book will help.

Graham W. Wall .   Holbeach Wildfowlers.

Introduction and Acknowledgments

This is a book about wildfowling, the last truly wild sport we have in this country. It traces my faltering steps into this strange, magical, and sometimes dangerous world inhabited by the wildest of our wildlife, cloying and all-pervasive mud, and silent treacherous tides. I soon discovered that it is not a sport for the rash and foolhardy, or one who judges the success of the activity by the size of the bag. Beyond the sea wall we encounter Nature in the raw, with all its grandeur and majesty, in all its moods.

The wildfowler must be content with meagre returns for considerable effort, be prepared to encounter hardship and physical challenge, and far more often than not, be content to witness the sights and sounds of the surroundings without ever raising the gun. However, in his or her mind's eye, the wildfowler can readily recall every successful shot, every hard-won bird brought to bag, and this only enhances the culinary pleasure when such a prize is served at dinner.

Like deer stalking in lowland woodlands or fly fishing for sea trout in the hours of darkness, the themes of my previous book, *'I'll be Back in an Hour'*, anyone engrossed in wildfowling cannot help but become a keen observer of Nature. However, the difference is that stalking and fly fishing normally take place inland, in a landscape influenced, if not actually shaped, by the hand of Man. By contrast, the human influence on the environment of the coastal wildfowler is puny.

For me, the wildfowling learning curve began on my first visit to one little patch of the only great wilderness area left in the British Isles, the saltmarshes and foreshore of our coastline, and this learning continues each time I rise at 'ungodly o' clock' on a winter's morning to cross the sea wall in the dark before dawn.

By its very nature, tales of my wildfowling makes this account rather more autobiographical than my previous book, but it couldn't be otherwise. Since the age of seven I have recorded my shooting forays, first as a family chore, then out of habit, and now out of the sheer pleasure of being able to turn back the pages of my Game Book and re-live past adventures.

Since the turn of the millennium, the handwritten entries have always stated that I was accompanied by my wife Pam, who was once described by Clarissa Dixon-Wright as an 'intrepid woman'. She has endured all the strenuous challenges of rising at 4 o' clock, three-mile forced marches along the sea wall in the pre-dawn dark, being blasted by storm force winds on an unsheltered foreshore, and sat through blizzards in the hope of meeting a low-flying skein of geese. All this without a word of complaint, except when I have had the temerity to suggest that she may like to have an odd lie-in and to give a dawn flight a miss!

She is a wildfowler, and this book is for her.

Robin Marshall-Ball
Westbury
2008

PART 1: the EARLY YEARS

CHAPTER 1   WILDFOWLER'S DAWN

The dreams of a five-year-old. . . .guns in the family. . . .first shot disaster. . . .a frozen thumb. . . .flying pigeons. . . .the Czech aristocrat.

The scene opens with a five-year-old throwing the sort of tantrum that only five-year-olds can throw.   Crashing around my bedroom whence I had been banished, slamming wardrobe doors, throwing toys about and kicking the floorboards   while at the same time maintaining a continuous stream of high-pitched invective about the gross unfairness of the planet, the house in which I lived, and my family. In particular, the rampant injustice meted out to me by my father and elder brother. From my bedroom window I watched through bitter tears of anger and frustration as they de-frosted the car and began packing it with boots, coats, cartridges and guns – they were going wildfowling. As it was a bitterly cold day in mid-December, I was considered neither old nor hardy enough to go with them but I, of course, thought otherwise.

After their departure calm returned to the household, aided by a bowl of mother's home-made soup and the permission to stay up for the wildfowlers' return, and I waited long into the hours of darkness for the sound of the Morris Oxford drawing up by the front of the house.   I held the door open to welcome them back, the two weary figures, their coats, hands and guns caked in mud, red-rimmed wind blasted eyes and cold-induced peaked expressions, they bore all the essential ingredients from which boyhood heroes are made, and the three feathered bundles they handed to me were prized beyond value.

Though now long past my bed-time, I could not wait till morning for an account of their adventures. Sitting around a blazing log fire holding steaming hot mugs cupped in their hands, they gradually thawed out while filling my imagination with bitter winds soughing over lonely marshland, of treacherous flooding tides, packs of duck appearing suddenly out of icy sleet showers, and long slogs over unforgiving mud. Eventually, before the warmth and gentle crackle of the log fire in a room filled with the fragrant smell of pine wood smoke, I was given their promise that one day I would follow in their footsteps down to the foreshore and become a wildfowler. I fell into a contented sleep to dream the dreams of all aspiring 'fowlers. Even now, more than half a century later, I still have the same dreams in the nights before we go in search of wild geese.

I was lucky to be born into a shooting and fishing family. My parents met in Calcutta in the 1930s, my father was an engineering officer in the merchant navy before he took a shore job with an oil company, and my mother the daughter of the Forestry Commissioner in Burma. During their time in India, spending weekends and holidays on 'shikar' became their normal mode of life and both my sister and brother (12 years and 6 years my senior

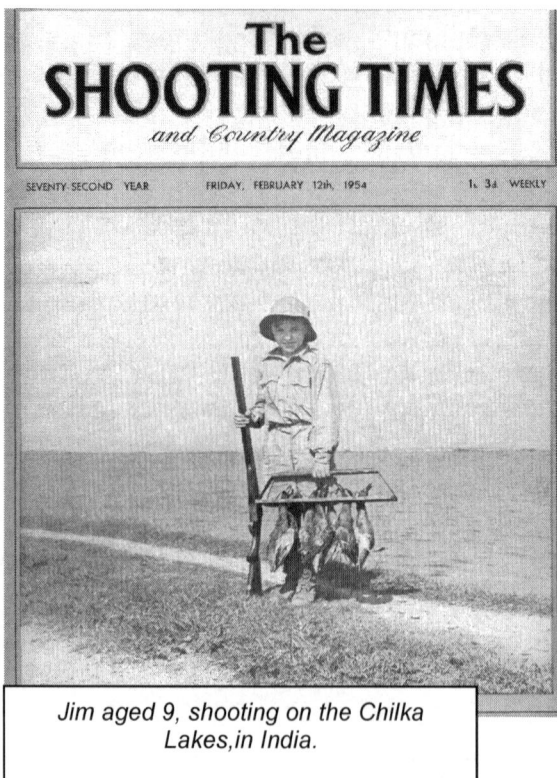

The
SHOOTING TIMES
and Country Magazine

SEVENTY-SECOND YEAR   FRIDAY, FEBRUARY 12th, 1954   1s 3d WEEKLY

Jim aged 9, shooting on the Chilka Lakes, in India.

respectively) were introduced to the shooting field in the Orissa jungles and the Chilka Lakes. With the fading days of the British raj the family moved back to Britain, settling in the soft rolling landscape drained by the River Teifi in west Wales. I was only eighteen months old when we settled in our new home, so despite my father being a 'Geordie' from South Shields and my mother's Scottish ancestry, it was only natural that I have come to consider myself to be Welsh through and through – if not by blood-line then certainly by osmosis through my skin, I absorbed the countryside, the culture, and the language. Following our settling in period, my father's leave ended and he returned to his job in India, he was to remain in this post until my late teens when he finally retired. Thus it was the beginning of a rather unusual pattern of contact with my father as he returned on leave for six months every two years. To modern society this may seem a very unsatisfactory arrangement, but in the early 1950s it was generally accepted as the norm for 'unaccompanied' employment overseas, particularly in the civil service, commerce, and the armed forces. Naturally, in my father's absence I looked to my elder brother for tutelage, mentoring and support through my early learning years.

Sporting guns were part of everyday life. In the days before heightened security and steel gun cabinets, the family's guns stood in their rack in the lounge without even a security chain to tie them together. During my father's absence the rack contained my mother's Webley & Scott boxlock ejector 16 bore and my brother Jim's Midland non-ejector 20. Both guns bought in Manton's gunshop in Calcutta in 1937, the 20 was originally the 'memsahib's' gun until Jim took it over. Alongside these two shotguns stood our .22 rimfire rifle, a very basic BSA Sportsman Single which was, however, superbly accurate, and my first airgun, a Diana No 1 which was loaded from the muzzle end and was horrendously inaccurate!. At these times there were two empty spaces in the rack that were filled whenever my father came back on leave, adding his Webley & Scott 12 bore and a Savage 15-shot .22 self-loading rifle, which he always referred to as his 'rabbit gun'. He never brought his big game rifles back on leave as there was no reason to do so, thus, and to my lifelong regret, I never got to see his John Wilkes .500 Nitro double rifle or the Rigby .30-06 bolt action.

Far from familiarity breeding contempt, the ready access to the family's guns engendered a respect for safety and safe handling that began as soon as each of the children was big enough to pick up their first toy gun. This was the source of some confusion and mirth when I began to play

A posed photo: Jim at 13 with the .20 bore and me aged 6 holding a borrowed .410 shotgun. I never got to fire it.

cowboys and Indians with my new-found friends from the local village – I could not bring myself to break the family taboo by pointing my cowboy pistol at them, so I quickly gained the reputation of being a hopeless shot!

Before I was given my first airgun, my prized possession was a double-barrelled cork-firing 'shotgun'. Made of die-cast metal, cocking the springs was a real trap for unwary little fingers, but nevertheless I learned, quite painfully at times, to handle it carefully and treat it with respect. To my young eyes it was a 'real' gun just like the other shotguns in the rack, and armed with this popgun I accompanied my mother or brother in little 'pot-hunting' walks along our lane or around the neighbouring fields. All the while I was under constant scrutiny for any lapses in safety in my handling of the gun, and I learned through instruction, observation and imitation. Rabbits were in plentiful supply and the occasional unwary pigeon came to hand, though at the time I could not understand why my own gun was so much less effective than their shotguns!

My first shot with a 'real' shotgun, the 20 bore, was a complete disaster! I had reached the milestone age of seven years old, the age at which Jim had taken his allotted place for a duck shoot on the Chilka Lakes near Calcutta. Shooting with the style and panache of his seniors, the other Guns stopped shooting to watch him, (you can imagine my father's feelings!) and his bag contained bar-headed geese, garganey, and cotton teal. With such a precedent before me, I was under considerable pressure. A target was pinned to the trunk of the large conifer that stood in front of the house and Jim measured thirty paces back to where I should stand. Carefully the barrels were checked and a cartridge loaded into the left barrel – I was to use the rear trigger as my finger could not yet reach the right barrel's front trigger . The gun is handed to me open, with trembling hands I close the breech, slip the safety off and mount it to my shoulder. From the base of the tree, I draw the bead up to the target, close my eyes, and pull the trigger. Of all the advice I had tried hard to heed, the one thing I had forgotten was to hold the stock tight into my shoulder. My cheek and shoulder were dealt such a severe blow that I nearly dropped the gun, and thrusting it back to my brother I fled into the house in a flood of tears with the gun's report and some quite uncharitable comments from Jim still ringing in my ears. I did not touch any gun for six months and although I was still very happy to accompany my elders on their walkabout forays, I flinched every time a shotgun was fired. I was very definitely 'gun-shy'.

My father arrived for a short stay. It was clear even to my young eyes that things were not right in my parents' relationship and his stay in the family home was only for the last two weeks of his leave. Goaded by my brother's taunts and criticisms, I was keen to redeem myself in the shooting field and made many overtures and requests for a .410 shotgun, all of which fell on deaf ears. Shortly before his departure, father handed me the 20 bore and two cartridges and casually told me that he'd noticed a pigeon flight -line over our orchard, and that I should to go and shoot one! There I stood on a cold January morning wrapped up in thick coat and scarf and holding an artefact I really feared using. This time there was no audience and no stream of advice. I go through the loading procedure – open the gun, peer down the barrels to check they are clear, load one cartridge, close the gun, check the safety is 'on', stand and wait, hoping secretly that no bird would fly by. Ten minutes later I was preparing to return to the house having successfully avoided the terrifying prospect of pulling the trigger when over the beech hedge at the far end of the orchard came a woodpigeon. Bracing myself for the ordeal, the safety was slipped off and the gun came to my shoulder. I tracked the bird with the bead and did the deed. The gun fired, the bird flared and retreated in a great hurry, leaving behind an exhilarated and almost euphoric little boy standing alone in the orchard, sniffing at the empty and still smoking cartridge case he had just extracted from his gun. No pain, no shock of bone-jarring recoil, just a huge sense of achievement. I discovered in that instant that there is a world of difference between shooting at static or moving targets. Quickly I reloaded and searched the sky for something else to shoot at, but a few minutes later I was called back to the house to be greeted by hugs and praise and many 'you-nearly-got-it' comments. Unbeknown to me, my father had been watching from an upstairs window, and after my shot he turned to Jim, 'I think that's cured Robin's problem,' he said, 'perhaps you'll have to use your mother's 16 bore from now on'.

For the remaining few days of my father's stay I spent many hours huddled against the trunk of an ancient bramley apple tree in a vain attempt to shoot a pigeon. Although I had pulled the trigger five more times, my shots had failed to connect and Jim was becoming concerned that I was using up his precious cartridge supply – after all, a box of twenty-five Eley '20 Gauge' cartridges cost fifteen shillings, the same price as three gallons of petrol! As a parting gift father gave Jim a box of 16 bore cartridges and two pigeon decoys, and for me there was my very own box of cartridges for the 20 bore. To me this was a symbolic gift – an acknowledgement that I had become a shotgun shooter. In addition, I was told that as the youngest shooting member of the family, the duty now fell to me to write up records of our outings in the family's game book, a habit that I have continued to this day. On his departure, father mentioned that he would take us wildfowling when he next returned, but though I did not know it at the time, I was not to see him again for seven years, and we never did manage to venture down to the saltings together.

My first pigeon, according to the old book lying on my desk as I type this page, came on the day my father sailed back to India from Southampton. We had seen pigeons congregating on the rape field of a nearby farm, and Jim was as keen to try out his new decoys as I was to have my first real shooting opportunity. We arrived at the field in the late morning of a bitterly cold January day, a heavy blanket of ominous yellow-grey clouds filled the sky and frost still crackled underfoot, making a silent approach impossible. A flock of around fifty pigeons clattered off the field when we appeared, and we quickly set about building our hide. The field was bounded on one side by a broken row of oak trees growing along the hedge line, and at the foot of the hedge was a shallow ditch, an ideal place for concealment. Jim placed the two decoys in front of our chosen position and we settled down to await the pigeons' return. It started to snow. Thick heavy flakes poured silently out of the overloaded sky, the largest making a slight 'clicking' sound on impact with the ground or vegetation around us, and there was no sign of any melting as our coats, the hide, and the field began to change colour.

The pigeons returned in one big flock. Appearing as swift ghostly shapes out of the swirling sky, they inspected our partially snow-covered decoys with some distain and settled in the far corner of the field. Some minutes later Jim decided to attempt a stalk, and after first warning me of the dire consequences of getting a snowflake in my barrels, he slithered through the hedge and crept away. Minutes passed, then suddenly there was the sound of two gunshots and birds were in the air. One turned, and passing over the decoys settled in an oak tree to my left. Desperately I tried to slip the safety catch off but my thumb was now too numb with the cold and it buckled each time I put pressure on it. Try as I may, the catch refused to slip forward. The pigeon remained on its branch, facing away from me with its head sunk into its chest and plumage fluffed out for warmth, it did not notice the hide and the small figure struggling with frozen glove-less fingers. At last, in desperation I pressed the gun to the tree trunk behind me and pushed gently. There was a quiet click as the catch moved, and within a few moments I was back in the hide stroking and admiring the first bird ever to fall to my gun. It was now snowing harder than ever, and when Jim appeared bearing gun and two pigeons, we spent some minutes looking for the decoys as they were now well buried in what had become a thick white field-sized blanket, before making tracks for home. Even with the heat of a blazing open fire and a large mug of hot soup, it took some time before feelings returned to my hands and for me to stop shivering, but I still made several trips to the kitchen to check that 'my' pigeon was still there!

In the remaining winter months my tally of pigeons had increased to five but still I could not hit a flying bird. Both Jim and mother frequently repeated the mantra of swinging through, giving the bird lead, shooting where the target is going to, and much other helpful advice, yet this only served to confuse me more. I had no idea where my shot was going when firing at a flying target, but it all became clear on a sunny morning in the first week of March. Tucked into the hedge overlooking the small rape field on our neighbour's farm, Jim had gone 'walkabout' while I was to shoot any pigeons that came to our two decoys. From the hide I saw a small flock, perhaps a dozen or so birds, cross the hedge to my right. It was obvious that they had no interest in the field and even less in the decoys as they flew past about thirty yards out from my hide. With the instruction 'pick on one and don't brown the flock' uppermost in my mind, I swung the gun onto the beak of the lead bird and fired. A pigeon fell out of the air, my first flying bird! To add to my amazement, it wasn't the one I had picked but the third in line. Over and over I re-lived the mental 'snapshot' picture one gets when the trigger is pulled and suddenly understood just how far in front of the bird I must swing the gun for a shot to connect. Some time later, a single pigeon appeared and flew the same route as the flock. With the image of my previous shot in my mind, I swung well ahead and fired. What had been in an instant before a strong-flying bird suddenly transformed itself into a neat ball which fell, in a shower of feathers, between the decoys. There was a shout of 'Good shot Rob!' from the far end of the field, Jim had returned and had seen it all. Laying the unloaded gun aside I rushed out to meet him. Shaking my hand, he spoke in his best feigned public school accent, 'I say old chap, damn fine shot, what?'

For the next three years all our shooting was confined to woodpigeons. My mother had not yet learned to drive a car and we were thus restricted to shooting within walking distance from our house. All the neighbouring farmers came to know us and we were given the freedom of their lands as we made our own little forays in an attempt to keep pigeons off their crops. How the world has changed, for what farmer in the present day would allow a thirteen and seven year old, both armed with shotguns, free range to wander and shoot pigeons where they will? The tenant farmers of the estate to the west of our home, however, were adamant that we were to confine our shooting activities strictly to crop protection. We did encounter the odd pheasant in our wanderings, but left them alone except when they strayed off the estate, but there is one pheasant story I reserve for another chapter.

I was ten years old when one morning there came a heavy knock on our front door. There stood what to me was a strange apparition. Tall and gaunt he was, dressed in a mixture of well-worn tweed and ex-army clothing, his manner was impeccably courteous and over a cup of tea he spoke to us in a slow and deep east European accent . Later, I heard all sorts of stories about this enigmatic owner of a small woollen mill in a nearby village, but it was generally accepted that he was a member of the Czech aristocracy who had fled his country with the coming of the Nazis or communism. But it was this first meeting with

Gustav Bridlik that was to change my life forever. Having previously shared some shooting land with my father, and understanding that my father's absence may put a limit on our shooting, on this occasion he had called to our house to seek mother's permission to widen our shooting horizons. He wanted to take us wildfowling.

PART 1: the EARLY YEARS

CHAPTER 2: .CARMARTHEN BAY.

An epic bus ride. . . .Laughrne Ferry – 'the Point'. . . .first camp. . . .new species. . . a car and freedom. . . .the Greener GP. . . .first duck in a storm. . . .creek crawling and 'cowboys'. . . . opening day camping. . . .the Geography teacher.

The bus conductor regarded us with curiosity as we stepped onto the red Western Welsh bus heading for Carmarthen. 'You got licenses for those then?' he asked as he eyed the shotguns we had carried onto his vehicle, gun sleeves were un-heard of in those days and our brown paper wrapping covered only the breech and triggers. The ten-shilling Post Office documents were duly produced to his satisfaction, and when we asked for return tickets to Llansteffan, his response was 'Oh, it's ducks you're after then is it?'. . . .'You must be the boys from Penyrallt,. . . .Mr Bridlik said you would be getting on, he's down the back of the bus'

Thus, at the start of the school Christmas holidays, began our first adventure with Gustav Bridlik. With mild weather forecast, Mother felt happier for us to spend the night in a tent even though it was December. The plan was to spend much of one day on the coast and camp overnight so that we could have a morning flight before returning home. We were on the 5.30 'workers' bus' heading towards the county town, where we would change busses at the depot and head out to Llansteffan and the estuary of the Taf as it enters Carmarthen Bay. Although it was still nearly two hours to dawn, the journey time and the two mile walk from the bus stop to our shooting ground meant that we would miss the morning flight, but arrive well before high tide at around 10.00am. The bus was crowded but we edged our way down the isle, past the other passengers huddled over their first Players Navy Cut or Woodbine of the day. With all windows closed, the dim interior lights made the inside of the vehicle look more like a Dickensian opium den than a commuter shuttle. We were frequently stopped by fellow travellers, questioned about our destination and quarry, and given much encouragement to 'get a bird for Christmas'. Perhaps of all the comments, the one that pleased me most was from an old man who, after learning of our mission, looked at me with narrowed appraising eyes and said. 'Oh, you're a wildfowler, then!' Although I had never seen, let alone shot at, any wildfowl, I felt that I had taken one step up in the shooting world.

Mr Bridlik (for that was how I always addressed him, even into my adulthood) had saved two places for us by piling coats, bags, tent, and other paraphernalia on two adjacent seats, and these items he now heaved onto the floor to give us room to sit. Then, after a friendly greeting and an estimate of our time of arrival, he stretched his legs into the isle and fell asleep. I was far too excited. Since the time of his first visit to our house, I had tried to read any wildfowling book I could lay my hands on, and although the Lonsdale Library's *Wildfowling* volume provided me with a textbook on the sport, it was Peter Scott's *'Wild Chorus'* and James Wentworth-Day's *'The Modern 'Fowler'* which really fired my imagination. From the small and limited pages of my *'Observer's Book of Birds'* I had memorised the characteristics of the duck I hoped to encounter and the many shore birds I hoped to see and hear for the first time. All through the journey I pestered Jim for recollections of his two forays to the coast with my father five years earlier, and his own excitement and anticipation kept us both chatting excitedly during both legs of the bus journey.

It was only when we changed busses in Carmarthen that I realised just how striking, and possibly alarming, our mentor may have appeared to others. We waited till the rest of the bus had emptied at the depot before disembarking. At well over six feet tall, each time he moved Mr Bridlik produced a sound effect similar to a set of heavy cow-bell wind chimes! Tied to every button on his thick and faded tweed jacket were saucepans, cooking utensils, a meths-burning cooker, and a net bag of tinned food. In one hand he carried an ancient double 12 bore hammer gun and the other held a large walking stick. On his back a huge ex-military rucksack contained blankets, groundsheet, and a small canvas tent, the poles of which were tied together and slung across his shoulder. We had much lighter burdens. Our own smaller bags contained our new-fangled sleeping bags recently bought for us by Mother, a thermos flask and water bottle and a few items of food in addition to gloves, extra clothing, and cartridges.

It was light by the time the bus dropped us off at the top of the steep hill just beyond Llansteffan, and we set out to walk the remaining distance along the minor lanes towards Laughrne Ferry, a wildfowling venue known to all who visited it as 'the Point'. Every now and then we paused, and where we could catch a glimpse, Jim and I would climb the hedge to look out over the wide expanse of Carmarthen Bay. Cresting the last rise, at last we could see our destination. Nestling under a steep bank on the opposite side of the River Taf was the small town of Laughrne, I was only later to learn of its fame through the writings of Dylan Thomas, where the town is thinly disguised as Llareggub in his classic 'Under Milk Wood'. Upstream to the right were bare mudflats edged by greenery, and to the left the far side of the widening estuary was bordered by the low sandhills of Pendine. Right before us lay a tapering finger of land pointing directly at Laughrne. On this little estuary began a learning process which continues to this day, it was to be the scene of many adventures in the years to come, and it was where the call of wildfowl and the smell of the saltmarsh first infected my blood.

We dropped our baggage in the lee of the hedge on the southern boundary in the last narrow field of the Point, where the stunted and wind-contorted bushes offered our camp some protection from onshore winds, we hastily untied our brown paper 'gun covers' and rummaged in our bags for cartridges. On the far side of the hedge the terrain fell away quickly to a strange flat land which at first appeared to be rough pasture, but from our vantage point I could see that it was dotted with little flashes of water and cut by a number of muddy channels which wound through the vegetation out to the mud and sand beyond. So this was the 'saltmarsh' that I had read so much about! As we watched, the river appeared to be widening and some floating objects were moving upstream. Silently, the tide was rising and covering the seaward mudflats. Our leader thought it was time to take our places before the anticipated flight began.

At the end of the field was a small grass-covered and hawthorn-fringed mound and it was to this that Mr Bridlik directed me, ' Tuck in behind the bushes and you can still get a good view all round', he advised, 'listen and watch

The view upstream from the 'mound'. Scene of my first wildfowling adventures at Laugharne

carefully, and I will shout if I see any duck coming your way!'. He rambled off to stand a short distance away, tucked behind some brambles and leaning against the corner of a roofless stone building which I was told was once the 'waiting room' when the ferry to Laughrne operated a century before. From this hide he could also keep an eye on Jim, whom he had sent down to the end of the point where the tidal scour had cut into the pasture to produce small cliffs and gullies. In this broken ground Jim could hide until the tide lapped at his feet, at which stage he would simply step up onto dry land and hide among the clumps of soft rush.

By 10.00am the whole estuary on either side of the Point was filled by a sheet of muddy silent water, but as the tide advanced to this height the air in all directions had become dotted with hundreds, perhaps even thousands, of birds. In this new and exciting world I often reached for my little Observer's Book, turning the pages frantically and trying to match the printed calls with the sounds I could hear. Curlew and redshank were easy and several small parties of these flew the short-cut across the Point to an upstream roost. Others followed the edge of the tide and several shots came from Jim's position. A ragged bunch of swift-flying birds approached unseen from behind and flashed over my head before suddenly scattering in a vertical climb when a shot rang out from our guide. As they flared I saw that they were 'duck-shaped' and by the size they could only have been teal. One little dot crumpled and fell near the stone ruin and some minutes later I was pleased to confirm my identification, though not by the comment that I must have been asleep!

Several small parties of duck did fly over the mound, but on each occasion I heard the shout of 'No!', - in the mild air and gentle wind they were well out of gunshot as they crossed the Point.   I saw a line of six or seven birds heading straight for me at a much lower level.   Rapid wingbeats, flying in line, they must be duck. This was my chance! I pressed myself further into the thorn bush and slipped the safety catch off, preparing to mount the gun, but just as I did so, one of the birds called. The loud and high-pitched *'t'keep. .t'keep'* did not match any of the duck calls I had tried to memorise, and the party of oystercatchers in their smart piebald uniforms and long bright orange bills sailed over my head as I lowered the gun and my heart rate began to subside.

The tide flight petered out and we were called together. Carefully I inspected both the mallard that Jim had shot and Mr Bridlik's teal as we set up camp. A flask of hot soup was produced and he began cooking a one-pot meal over a hissing Primus stove. The early morning start, the excitement of the sights, sounds, and smells of the foreshore, and the prospect of shooting to come, all served to sharpen our appetite. No banquet could have tasted better than the simple meat and potato stew we consumed voraciously in the open air with the salt-laden breeze ruffling our hair. Mr Bridlik wrapped himself in his oilskin coat and settled back for a siesta while we performed our 'washing-up duties' by giving the pan, bowls and utensils a perfunctory wipe with a damp cloth. Still too excited to have any thoughts of rest, we earnestly recounted our morning's experiences while scanning the skies for birds on the move. Just occasionally, a small trip of duck or group of other wildfowl would cross the Point and by the time our leader woke up, Jim and I were standing 'armed sentry' positions some twenty yards on either side of our camp.

Light was just beginning to fade when we again took up our positions for the evening flight, though with the tide now far out, Jim had ventured further away from dry ground and was crouched among the seaweed-covered rocks towards the river channel. That evening I fired my first cartridge at wildfowl. A loose party of duck came from the seaward side of the mound and passed over me at a height of around thirty-five yards. At my shot they flared before disappearing into the upstream gloom and though I willed it desperately, no bird fell. In my heart I knew that with all the excitement I had fired haphazardly into the bunch and not picked on a bird, and it was the only chance I had.

Though Mr Bridlik had not fired a shot, Jim had again been successful and back at the camp by the light of a small hurricane lamp I closely inspected yet another species I had only previously read about, a wigeon. After another one-pot meal of sausages, bacon and beans, fatigue rapidly overcame us boys, we crawled into the tent, struggled into our sleeping bags, and were instantly asleep. Much later, after I had passed through the 'deep sleep' phase, I was awoken on a number of occasions by the whicker of wings and the bubble and whistle of wigeon as they flighted overhead in the darkness, a sound which I find as exciting now as I did during that first night.

I used another precious cartridge on the dawn flight, a despairing parting shot at a small flock of teal that flashed past me in the early morning light but again my shot failed to connect. The challenge of shooting pigeons is that they are so manoeuvrable, duck, I was beginning to realise, are generally straight-line fliers, but they move much faster than pigeons! Both Jim and Mr Bridlik had added a wigeon each to the bag, and although I had failed to contribute, I began asking earnest questions about when we could come wildfowling again as we struck camp and began the weary trek back to the bus stop. Apparently I slept most of the way home.

We made two more epic bus-borne expeditions to the Point in the following January and again in late September, and despite using six cartridges I had yet to shoot a duck! However, two factors now were to revolutionise our wildfowling. Mother had passed her driving test and Jim was learning to drive. Suddenly we were independent of bus timetables and had become much more mobile.

With this came mother's stated intention to come wildfowling with us, and so for Jim's seventeenth birthday he graduated to a 12 bore. Looking back, we missed a few real bargains in the search for one suitable. In 'Jack Alma's' shop in Llandysul we inspected a double hammerless 3" gun by Tolley, but Jim was put off by the fact that, although it had just been re-proofed, the barrels were still 'in the white' and had not been re-blacked. The asking price was £25 and it was turned down. Finally, even though it meant he was restricted to single shots, he opted for a new gun. At a cost of £21.19s.6d, the Greener 'GP'12 bore arrived, and a sortie to the marsh was quickly organised. I retained the 20 bore and mother was to use the 16.

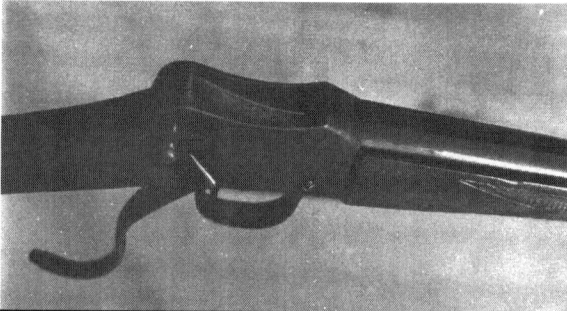

Jim's Greener GP. immensely strong but a bane when using damp and swollen cartridges!

This time we encountered real 'fowling weather'. Daylight was being dragged reluctantly into the sky through a thick blanket of rain clouds as I stood on the lee side of the mound, collar turned up and shoulders hunched to shelter from the strong wind and heavy rain showers being driven onshore. Mother was tucked in against the ruined stone wall of the 'waiting room', Jim had stumbled off in the pre-dawn darkness to hide in a creek on the upstream saltings, and Mr Bridlik, whom we had collected in the early hours, crouched behind a tree trunk that had been stranded by the tide at the tip of the Point. In the slowly strengthening light, parties of duck disturbed by the wind-whipped waters of the rising tide hurtled downwind over the Point to seek more shelter upstream, and dimly against the wind I heard the occasional 'pop' of a gunshot from Jim, the GP was in action.   Two trips of fowl had come past me, but my reactions had been far too slow to catch up with them. I turned to face the wind, hoping to give myself more warning of the next lot, and thus more time to prepare for a shot. Over the buffeting of the wind I heard a faint shout from mother who was watching upstream from her stone wall shelter, and I spun round to see a large group of duck beating upwind towards me through the veil of rain. Throwing the gun to my shoulder I swung ahead of the lead bird and fired. Though I could now reach the front trigger and had loaded two cartridges into the 20 bore, I stared upwards in wonderment and delighted disbelief, completely forgetting the second shot! Two duck were dropping out of the sky! Certainly not the one I had picked, but the one behind the lead bird and another I had not noticed. What added to my excitement was that I had shot a wigeon, which fell at my feet, and a teal which had dropped into some thistles behind where I stood. Mother rushed over and after an embarrassing congratulatory hug (what wildfowler, I thought, could be hugged by his mum and still retain any 'marsh-cred'!) she explained that she had called a warning when she saw two parties of duck approach my position, but by the time I fired they had joined up. Hence the two species that now lay in the grass at my feet and were taking up so much of my admiring attention that I missed a number of other opportunities before I turned back to face the wind. Again in my mind's eye I re-lived the sight picture at the moment of firing to gauge how far in front of a bird I needed to swing the gun, but these birds were flying upwind!

Downwind birds were very much faster and I doubled the forward allowance for my next two shots, but still failed to connect. A heavy rain squall had just passed when three more duck came in from the sea. Picking on one, in desperation I put what I thought was a ridiculous amount of sky between the bead and the bird as I swung ahead and fired. The wigeon cart-wheeled out of the air to hit the wet mudflats below the mound, sliding several feet before coming to rest. Scrambling down to marsh level I picked up a gnarled stick from the tideline at the foot of the mound and set off to retrieve the bird. This was very scary. The first time I had set foot on estuary mud and visions of being swallowed by quicksand caused me to move slowly one pace at a time. At this slow progress my boots were sinking into the ooze to well above my ankles and each step raised my fear level. There was a shout, and turning I saw Mr Bridlik's head appear on the crest of the mound. 'The mud is ok here' he shouted, 'but just walk quickly and you'll be alright!' I turned, and using the stick for support ,extricated my boots from their craters and tried to 'skate'. It worked! In no time I found myself back on the mound, breathless from exertion but proudly holding a very muddy drake wigeon. Mr Bridlik solemnly shook my hand, 'Look at your boots!' pointing to the quantity of estuary mud still clinging to both my boots and most of my trousers, 'Now, you are a real wildfowler!

In all the years we came to this venue, it was one of the best morning flights we experienced on the Point, with all four of us contributing to the total bag of nine birds. Our plan was to stay all day but the scything wind and driving rain had affected all of us, I felt chilled to the bone and though I tried hard to disguise the fact so we could carry on, I had begun to shake quite uncontrollably! Jim wasn't in a much better state so we decided to pack up and head for home, basking in the knowledge that with our new mobility, we could return to the foreshore as often as we wished.

On four more occasions during that winter our black Ford Consul was parked up on the farm track leading to the Point. Often we found other cars parked there , this was, after all, a well-known wildfowling venue, and for the first time we witnessed what was later called 'marsh cowboy' behaviour. The duck had become 'marsh wise' and avoided crossing the Point, or if they did so, they flew at great height yet they were still greeted with gunshots. In order to intercept them when they were at a reasonable range, we had to get out onto the marsh well away from the higher ground. So, at Jim's suggestion and under his guidance, I had my first taste of 'creek crawling'. It was a steep learning curve. Half way along the Point we would turn right and drop down, first onto a narrow strip of short-cropped grazing marsh, then a further step down to the proper salt marsh. This was a wide belt of soft rush and coarse vegetation between which the summer cattle had left deep hoof-marks in soft , sticky, and very smelly mud which sucked and dragged at your boots, particularly it seemed, in the pre-dawn dark when you were in a hurry! Beyond this was the spartina marsh through which wound the deep creek and all the little side gullies which we used for concealment. I learned to use a stick as a probe to identify and avoid really soft mud, how to wedge a piece of driftwood across a gully to make a rudimentary seat, and learned to peer through, rather than over, the spartina to watch approaching birds. In addition, I quickly came to accept that when sitting in such an environment, mud gets everywhere – all over your hands and clothing, on your gun, even into your sandwiches and coffee! Jim felt he was rather better prepared for this 'mud-larking' as he had bought a green full-length all-rubber ex-army tank suit. Performing some incredible contortions, he would struggle to put this on over his normal shooting clothing and would enjoy a mobile sauna while walking onto or off the marsh. I tried it once, and made up my mind there and then never to join the Tank Regiment.

He had also learned to always carry a ramrod. These were the days before plastic waterproof cartridge cases. When paper cases became damp – an inevitable consequence of sitting for hours in a muddy creek – the paper swelled so that the extractor on his Greener GP jammed and refused to extract a spent cartridge. On one occasion he was hiding in a deep creek, surrounded by about two hundred wigeon grazing happily of the saltmarsh vegetation, while he silently and desperately tried to remove an empty cartridge from his gun! Though a classic and robustly-built shotgun, the GP lasted only until inexpensive and reliable Spanish guns began arriving on our shores.

One evening we were sitting in our usual creek hides. Though it had rained in the late afternoon, under a blustery westerly wind that hissed through the spartina and dried out the bunches of samphire at my elbow, the sky had cleared to a bright sunset. Looking to the west and into the yellow sky, in the distance I saw a ragged line of perhaps fifty or so birds flying inland over the hills behind Laughrne. Their calls, which in later years I likened to the sound of squeaky supermarket trolley wheels, came to us down the wind, and we both felt a surge of excitement we had not experienced before. Even though the sound was new to us, we knew in an instant that they were geese! Mr Bridlik had often regaled us with tales of shooting geese on the Point in years gone by, but we had neither seen nor heard these mystical birds in all our outings. This occasion turned out to be the only time we ever encountered geese in Carmarthen Bay, but the magic of their music made an indelible impression in my mind.

At the start of the next season, a new tradition was established which lasted until I graduated as a teacher and left Wales for a teaching post in England. Over the summer we had acquired a large ex-army ridge tent, and using this as a base, for the next decade we would welcome the dawn of each September 1st on the foreshore. The pattern was quickly established. Arriving to set up camp in the last days of August, we would spend the pre-season days noting the changes in the mudflats, creeks, and river channels, watching the tides and the flight-lines of wildfowl. As well as the resident duck, we had also discovered that early-season curlew and redshank, fresh from their inland breeding grounds, were tasty table birds as well as testing targets. Mother would assume the role of Camp Manager and Head Chef, detailing us off to forage for water, kindling, and firewood between our reconnaissance sorties while she prepared food and drink. After the meal, washing-up and other chores were allocated. Before dawn on the 1st we would be out to our shooting positions, and at a more sensible hour Mother would saunter down to the edge of the foreshore, gun in hand in case any wildfowl happened to fly by. To any other shooter she must have presented a disconcerting spectacle. A lady of short and dumpy stature, her 'wildfowling kit' consisted of short 'ladies' rubber gardening bootees, a faded tweed skirt topped by numerous jumpers, over which she always wore a beige gabardine mackintosh tied about the waist with baler cord – the belt had been lost in the mists of time. Each coat pocket held a handful of cartridges and for some unaccountable reason, she always carried a pair of secateurs! To us wildfowlers far out on the saltmarsh, caked in mud and facing intrepid conditions, this seemed to be a very 'laid-back' approach, but much to our amazement she still managed to shoot a respectable number of duck! Also much to our puzzlement, she invariably fired both barrels of her gun, even if a single bird had flown over and she had killed it with the first barrel! Among my wildfowling friends it became her 'signature', and on a number of occasions when we heard two distant rapid shots from the edge of the saltings, a call would come from a nearby creek, 'Rob! Your Mum's moved again!'

Of two life-long friends, the brothers Raymond and John Jones, more will be written in the next chapter describing our village gang, but mention must be made here that the September camp saw their introduction to wildfowling. In later years, before we were old enough to drive , when Jim had departed to London and Mother was otherwise unavailable, it was their father Dai Jones who acted as taxi driver to ensure the 'opening day' tradition was maintained for us three boys.

Over the three seasons we had been visiting Laughrne Ferry, we had witnessed an increase in shooting pressure. On one occasion we arrived late and counted ten other Guns spaced out along the length of this small peninsula. Some, much to our disgust, shooting at anything that flew and at any range. Thus, except in rough weather, all wildfowl gave the Point a very wide berth, and thankfully these conditions also tended to keep the 'cowboys' away. Except for the opening-day camp, we began to confine our visits to weekdays when gales were forecast, and in subsequent years we still occasionally enjoyed the luxury of having the marsh to ourselves in driving rain, howling winds, and heavy snow showers!

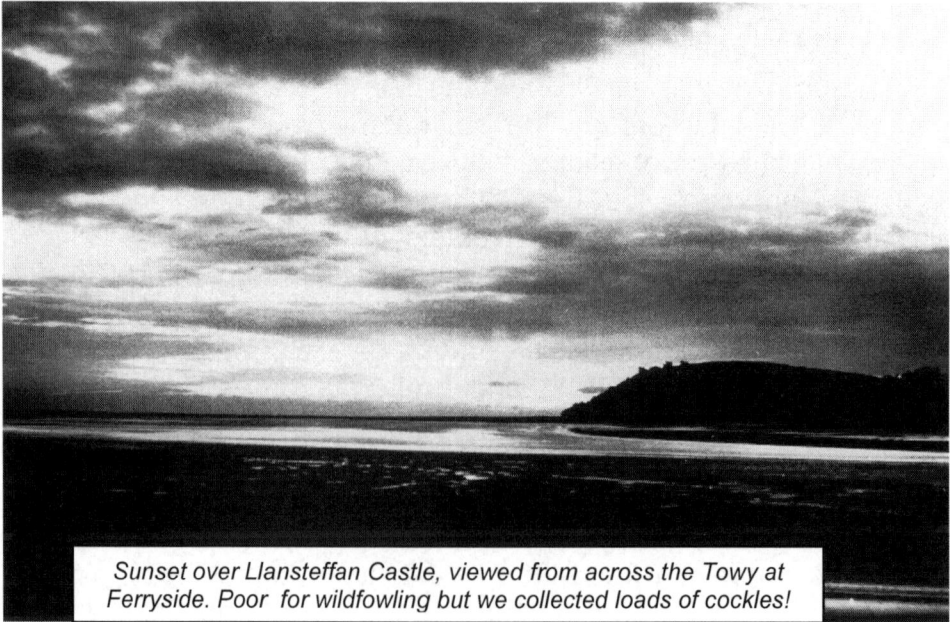

Sunset over Llansteffan Castle, viewed from across the Towy at Ferryside. Poor for wildfowling but we collected loads of cockles!

We needed to explore other wildfowling venues so Jim and I spent much time poring over Ordnance Survey maps of Carmarthen Bay. Ferryside, on the east bank of the Towy proved to be of little use for wildfowling, but we did return home with a bucket-full of cockles each time we ventured out onto the sands. Far more promising were the wide saltmarshes on the south bank of the Taf estuary at Pendine. Here the problem was that a large area of the sand dunes above high water mark was controlled by the army as a firing range, and on several occasions we had to abort our mission when we found warning flags hoisted and road gates locked.

I was twelve and in the second year in the 'big school' in Llandysul when a new geography teacher arrived. Although this new teacher habitually sat fiddling with the gas taps on his desk while he spoke to us, with his full beard, sparkling aquiline eyes, and ready smile, Tom Vaughn-Jones brought the subject to life through his vivid descriptions and sense of humour. He was the inspiration that led me in later life to a geography teaching career. In addition, he was a keen angler and, during his time as an undergraduate in Aberystwyth University, also a keen wildfowler. I talked about my own adventures, the over-shooting we were now witnessing, and our quest for new ground. At the end of one class he called me back to show me a large-scale map of the estuary he had shot over. 'This is where you should park', he said, marking a small cross with his pencil, 'you'll need to walk down to this bridge and then upstream along the railway line to about here', another cross. '. . .lots of wigeon and quite a few geese' he concluded. 'Now, you'd better get to your next class – oh, you can take the map'. Try as I may, I could not focus my mind on the intricacies of the Latin ablative absolute during the next lesson, after all, my geography teacher had casually mentioned the magic word 'geese', and this single word had completely destroyed all attempts at academic concentration!

I stole a surreptitious look at the map on my lap under the desk, and saw the words 'Dyfi Estuary'.

CHAPTER 3: THE VILLAGE GANG

Penyrallt Mansion. . . .language problems. . . .gang members and activities. . . private fishing. . . summer camps. . . .first shots and the quest for guns. . . .'Bert'. . . .tales of the riverbank. . . .mother's duck. . . .pheasants in snow. . . .'we three'.

When my parents decided to return from India to settle in Britain, they spent a short leave house-hunting around the Lake District, and apparently almost bought a house just outside Penrith. After all, it was a stone's throw across the Pennines to father's family in Tyneside, and in a remote and beautiful part of the countryside. They returned to India thinking that the purchase of the house was proceeding, only to be told on arrival that the whole thing had fallen through as the vendor had changed his mind! Thus, six months later my mother came back to the UK with instructions to explore other rural areas. Guided by the details of rural properties supplied to her by a national

A view of Penyrallt from the east side. My home until I left Wales for a teaching career in England

estate agent, in the course of her travels she ended up one night in a hotel in Cardigan. On the following morning she took a walk along the High Street, and a property advertised in the window of a small local estate agent caught her eye. She immediately arranged to view the property that day. Twenty miles upstream of Cardigan, one mile outside a small village, the house had been built in the mid-1800s by the High Sherriff of Carmarthen. All the woodwork in the interior was solid Burmese teak, a huge 'selling point' considering my mother's parentage, and the house stood in its own five acres of ground which included tennis courts, an extensive orchard, a paddock and stabling for horses. All the amenities, is seemed, of our home in India. The sale was agreed there and then, and some months later we moved into Penyrallt Mansion. I was eighteen months old when we moved in, and it was my home until I fledged and left the family nest to follow my teaching career in England.

From the start it was a curious existence. My sister Betty was attending a boarding school in North Wales, Jim had remained in India with Father - he was to follow on two years later when Father came on leave, which left my mother and a toddler rattling around this large house like loose peas in a pod! It must have been a real culture shock for my mother – without the team of servants she was accustomed to in India, the upkeep of the house took a great deal of her time and I was generally left to my own devices until Jim arrived. Before I reached school age I had the freedom to explore the grounds and surrounding fields, build dens, climb trees, and learned to catch trout by hand in the little stream below the house. With Jim's return came the guns, and from then on both shooting and fishing became a natural part of our lives.

Only when I began attending Brynsaron County Primary School did I meet any boys of my own age, and initially there were basic difficulties - for a start we spoke in different languages, and for the first two years of schooling, lessons were also taught in Welsh. In order to get along with my new-found friends, and to understand what was going on in class, I learned to speak Welsh very quickly!

Perhaps a word of explanation is needed here. One of the peculiarities of rural Wales is that there are so many surnames common to large proportions of the population, Jones, Evans, Davis, Williams etc., that they tend to be ignored. A person is therefore most usually referred to either by their first name or surname and the name of their *house*, or if this is not practical, by the occupation. Thus my circle friends first forged in primary school included Elgan *Maesyfelin*, Derrick *Dolwerdd*, Len Cole, Terry *Pencnwc*, and three brothers living in *Green-meadow,* Raymond, John, and Geraint. In keeping with this, I was (and occasionally still am) referred to as Robin *Penyrallt.* As we

Sliding on a frozen pond, members of our village gang.
L to R; Geraint and Raymond 'Greenmeadow', Elgan 'Maesyfelin'
and Derrick 'Dolwerdd'

grew up together there was no 'gang culture' as we have come to understand it today, just a bunch of friends, inseparable at weekends and school holidays. Occasionally we would board the bus to visit the 'big town', Carmarthen, and while there spend much time in the rod and gun shops, particularly 'Darks' tiny gunshop tucked away in the back streets near the market. Here we could sit for hours and hear tales of 'posh' pheasant shoots in the Towy valley, goose shooting on Tregaron Bog, and the latest information on duck numbers in the estuary. Though our custom seldom amounted to anything more than purchasing the odd tin of airgun pellets, we were always made welcome in this dark and dusty gunsmith's workshop.

At other times we would explore the small stream that ran, gurgling and chattering, through the village on its way to the Teifi. We wandered upstream at will along its course, trotting a worm here and there for the small trout hiding in its little pools and deep under-cuts, and casting a novice and clumsy fly across the occasional larger pools and the concrete 'salmon boxes' at Glynderi. For the fishing was free, so we came to know every nook and cranny of this dancing and sparkling little stream, learning where to find fish in every water condition from full roaring liquid chocolate spate to its 'summer bones' trickle.

The River Teifi was a different matter. For us village lads the only available fishing was within the boundary of the railway property where the line crossed the river. This black-painted steel construction was known as 'Pont Coch' (red bridge) after its initial colour scheme when the line was laid to link Newcastle Emlyn with Llandysul and onward to Carmarthen. All the riverbank on either side of this little strip was strictly private and watched by the riparian owner from his farmhouse on the hill. Stepping foot along the riverbank beyond the railway boundary would bring swift retribution, so, for the hours of daylight at least, we fished in a very confined space. Later, when we began fly-fishing into the hours of darkness for sea trout, this boundary became very blurred, but I perhaps should not dwell too much on this theme. Happily, for the present generation of village youths, all the fishing rights are now owned by Llandysul

Angling Club and access to fishing is now freely, and legally, available. Even fifty years later, as I stand at the top of the Dol Watts beat on a July evening, with swifts screaming about me in the golden light and the two rusting and derelict steel columns of the old bridge standing stark out of the water a few yards upstream, I find myself casting a furtive and guilty glance up to the farmhouse as I quietly set up my fly rod. Despite having the club permit and licence safely tucked into my waistcoat, old habits still die hard!

Of our group of friends, it was Raymond and John who were most deeply committed to both fishing and shooting. Some of our fishing adventures in the pursuit of sewin (sea trout) I have described in the companion volume to this book, '*I'll be Back in an Hour!*,' and

Two brothers and my lifelong shooting and fishing partners, John and Raymond Jones

to this day we always fish with Raymond whenever we return to the Teifi Valley. Each summer holiday their father Dai would take the three of us to some remote spot, where he would help us set up camp and then leave us to our own devices for a week or two, visiting us every other day to check that all was well. Armed with air rifles and fishing rods, we would attempt to live off the land, although we also had a plentiful supply of 'emergency rations'. On the heather moorland at Ty Coch we saw our first red and black grouse, though only closely-stalked rabbits featured on our log-fire menu, in the deep wooded valley of Cwm Cerrig we dined on small trout and pigeons, and at Llanfihangel we caught small sea trout to grill over the open fire. Where the opportunity arose, the odd few potatoes and other vegetables were quickly and silently gathered at night from the edge of any nearby fields, and these fruits of the land were supplemented by sausages and baked beans. Occasionally other friends would join us, but it was always us three that formed the core of 'adventurers' each year.

By the time we had reached 'double figures' in age, neither Raymond nor John had fired a shotgun, but hearing my tales of wildfowl and pigeon shooting with Jim, they were keen to try. One Saturday they arrived at my house just as I was taking the 20 bore out to dissuade the jackdaws from nesting in the kitchen chimney. Standing on the raised bank behind the house and full of authority and new-found importance, I talked them both (quite unnecessarily!) through the safety procedures, shooting a hapless jackdaw as part of my demonstration! It was then John's turn, but fearing the recoil he handed the gun on to his elder brother. Another bird appeared and Raymond fired. The bird flew off unscathed but with the delighted smile and sparkling eyes of achievement, the shooter turned to us declaring 'Diawl! That was easy - there's no kick at all!' Bolstered by this information, John fired the next shot at a pigeon that was well beyond range, but nevertheless it was a moving target, and the shot did not have the shoulder-wrenching effect he had feared. Like my experience three years earlier, taking their first shot at a moving target had made the breakthrough. For the next year or two, both brothers desperately saved pocket and paper-round money in their quest to buy their own shotguns.

I also became very interested and involved in the quest, and over this period we encountered some memorable guns. Small-bore shotguns were rare indeed, and 12 bores were viewed from the perspective that the boys would 'grow into them' as they reached teenage years. Within their very limited budget ,some very strange weapons were on offer. Behind every farmhouse door, it seemed, stood a loaded shotgun of indeterminate age and lacking several decades of care and maintenance. A virtual conveyor-belt of these rusty and decrepit hammer guns passed before our eyes and we gazed in wonder at both man's ingenuity and his complete disregard to personal safety. Where ribs had sprung off the barrels, they were tied back down with tight windings of copper wire. Where holes appeared in severely corroded barrels, they were promptly covered with tin-plate cut and shaped out of a baked bean tin, or filled with solder – the really good repairers had the gunsmithing skills to braze over the offending holes. Broken or cracked stocks were bound together with string or had metal plates covering the break, and often the gun's muzzles were so thin as to feel very sharp to the unwary finger. Raymond was offered one venerable double hammer gun that had diamond-shaped muzzles – they had been squashed in transit by having a sack of potatoes dropped onto them in the tractor. This presented no problem to the seller, who promptly knocked them back into almost circular shape with a heavy spanner! . Asking around the village for any guns for sale, we got word from one local farmer to meet him in the village pub so that we could inspect the gun he was prepared to sell. It was an old and very pitted hammer gun, with a brass strengthening plate on the cracked stock and muzzle metal so thin as to be razor sharp. The asking price of £5 was more than Raymond could afford so he asked for time to consider. After the farmer departed, old Will, sitting in his customary seat in the snug called us over, and waving his pipe in the air he declared 'Don't buy that gun, boys!, the barrels are too strained'. Thinking there was something about the condition of the neglected barrels we had not noticed, we asked for an explanation and he replied 'He keeps on shooting at things that are too far away, its ruined the gun!'

All these guns had one thing in common. With complete and heroic disregard to personal safety, the owners invariably declared that the weapon was still in regular use, and that they were hard-hitting and sure killers of anything they were pointed at, at whatever distance! Thankfully, Dai was an RAF armourer in the last war and he vetoed the purchase of such weapons, thereby allowing his sons to grow to maturity with all their limbs intact and fully functioning!

Eventually, the brothers acquired single barrel 12 bores which seemed to be in rather better condition than any of the double hammer guns they had been offered. John's first gun was a recently imported single 'semi-hammerless' model of Spanish origin marketed under the 'Denhill' brand. It must be remembered that this was in the era before AyA guns appeared on the scene, the first gentle warning ripple before the tidal wave of inexpensive Spanish and Italian shotguns that was to sound the death-knell of most English gunmaking firms. It was a soundly built and simple top-lever shotgun which, contrary to expectation, did not work loose too quickly. Its only disadvantage lay in its light weight , it kicked like a mule even with the Page-Wood 'Anti-Recoil' cartridges he sometimes used.

Raymond's gun was quite different, and for reasons beyond all logic it was christened 'Bert'. A bolt-actioned shotgun mounted on a rough-hewn stock, it must have been converted from a military weapon around the turn of the 20th century. No proof marks could be found on the metalwork, yet the barrel walls were thick enough to inspire confidence and over the years all manner of cartridges have been fired through this gun to very great effect. There was no choke restriction at the muzzle end of its 30" barrel, yet it seemed to be so effective at prodigious ranges that we concluded, contrary to all known laws of ballistics, that the shot pattern must first spread out and then converge again! By this time I had graduated to the 16 bore, and thus armed the three of us began to explore new ground. If the fishing on the Teifi was tightly controlled and beyond our legal access, Raymond and John *Green-meadow* were friendly with the riverside farmers and we quickly gained permission to shoot over their land. Not only did this give us access to much more pigeon shooting, but also we had leave to walk the riverbank and stalk the small ponds for duck. As the year slowly closed down for winter, many Saturdays would see us meeting at Pont Coch (the railway bridge) to work our way upstream in a search for mallard. In time we came to know their favoured resting places, and our tactics evolved - making detours so that we converged on a backwater or eddy from different directions simultaneously to try to get into range before any duck were flushed. Most times we drew blank and duck were few and far between, and a mallard to take home after walking several miles was a hard worked-for prize indeed. Some distance upstream of the bridge is a large, deep, and famous pool, and after the end of the fishing season, when disturbance from anglers ceased, it became our wildfowl 'hotspot'. In addition, the river's long and smooth glide down to the pool was fringed with a line of riverbank willow whose branches trailed and roots stepped into the river. The small eddies behind the willow screen produced many little secluded resting places which often held a duck or two when the river was not too high. Mallard were our main quarry, but in times of cold weather when duck numbers often increased, we sometimes encountered teal, leaping into the air from the most unlikely little ditches and partly-frozen ponds and taking us completely by surprise . On one occasion John returned from an upstream loop, we had heard a shot and saw, as he approached, that he was carrying a bird. He came up to us and handing it to me asked, 'Rob, what make of duck is this?' It was the first tufted duck any of us had seen.

Upstream from Pont Coch on a winter's day when we saw many teal

In the high summer we would spend many days crouching in nettle-infested hedge-side hides overlooking harvested corn stooks in the short drying period before the farmer's machines moved in to carry their harvest back to the barns. Bags were not enormous and my first 'double figure' bag of pigeons came on a sultry August day on Tan Coed farm as the machines began gathering the crop from the far end of the field. Later in the season, we would walk the steep bracken banks and small spinneys above Bercoed Isaf farm for a chance of an odd pheasant before the winter set in and we turned our attention to the duck on the river. Intertwined with these activities were our efforts with rod and fly line in the hours of darkness in order to come to terms with the sewin run.

At the tail end of a summer spate we decided to take up our spinning rods and try for sewin as the river was fining down. Mother decided to accompany us on this jaunt, bringing her gun along in case 'anything flew by'. She stood on the parapet of the bridge with the 20 bore over her arm, while under the bridge the water swirled and gurgled around the bridge supports, and despite trying all manner of spinners, we remained fish-less. Two gunshots, and having dropped our rods, we climbed the embankment onto the railway line only to see her gather a mallard that had fallen between the rails. After many congratulatory remarks we returned to our fishing, dimly aware that another adult angler, walking up from the gorge, had engaged my mother in conversation.

A few days later, Mother and I were shopping in our local market town of Llandysul when we were accosted by Willy *Half- Moon.* As well as being the manager of Pegler's Grocery Store in the High Street, Willy was also the landlord of the Half Moon Hotel, and an acknowledged expert in both angling and shooting. 'Good morning Mrs MB!' he greeted us with his usual cheerfulness, 'I hear you shot a mallard out of season the other day!' Mother was evidently embarrassed by this revelation, and begged for further details. 'That man you spoke to, when you confessed the duck was out of season and asked him not to breathe a word to anyone, . . .do you know who you were speaking to?' he queried. Mother pleaded ignorance. With his characteristic smile, Willy filled in the details to the horrified culprit, 'You were talking to the Deputy Chief Constable of Carmarthenshire Police!'. With such a lawless parent, what chance did I have?

Run the clock on a few years. Jim was now an undergraduate in Birkbeck College in London where he was reading 'Fine Arts', and only returned during the holidays. One Christmas break he returned, and determined to get the 'smoke' out of his lungs, picked up his Greener and the pigeon decoys and marched out of the house with the declared intention of shooting a few pigeons. A few hours later he returned. Crestfallen and quiet, he explained that at last he had been accosted by the estate's Gamekeeper, accused of poaching pheasants, and informed that legal proceedings were sure to follow. Mother became very distressed and had to lie down on the settee. Unwisely she asked where I was. 'Oh, Robin's down at the stream trying to shoot a salmon' was the casual reply that threw her into further paroxysms!

When calm was restored it turned out that the gamekeeper's inspection of Jim's bag revealed only five pigeons and some home-made decoys, but nevertheless a few weeks later, after Jim had returned to college, we received notification of impending prosecution. By now it had snowed and our grounds lay under a cold white blanket throughout the frost-filled days. I had been injured playing rugby and was hobbling around on crutches, but nevertheless I was awoken one morning with the sound of gentle hammering, and the call up to my bedroom to get my camera kit ready. The glass case containing two stuffed

Pheasants out of a glass case and posing in the snow!

pheasants had been dismantled and the birds removed. On Mothers instructions I placed these stuffed birds in the snow at various locations within our grounds, and took photographs of them from a variety of angles. When the prints were returned, a few that included the house in the background were selected for inclusion in her letter to the estate owner. The tone of her letter was one of high and haughty indignation. 'How dare you accuse my son of poaching your pheasants. . .as you can see from the enclosed photographs we have plenty of our own. . . . should you ever need any for your own Shoot, we would be happy to supply your needs from our own surplus stock!' Although thankfully our offer was never taken up, some weeks later we received notification that charges had been dropped.

With Jim's absence, Raymond, John, and I became an inseparable shooting team in our forays along the Teifi and further afield, and to the Point at Laughrne Ferry. We were 'going solo', though for reaching venues beyond our walking distance we were still dependent on transport laid on by my mother or their father.

Time has rolled on a further half century since the trio began shooting and fishing together. Twenty years ago John moved to Ireland, but in settled July evenings each year Pam and I share the Teifi riverbank with Raymond as sewin begin to awaken from their daytime torpor, and together we hear the magical sky-filling music of wild geese on the Scottish foreshore in the dark days of January.

CHAPTER 4:   The DYFI ESTUARY

Summer reconnaissance. . . .opening day. . . .the improbable fish. . . .the big freeze. . .goose in the fog. . . .a very silly idea. . . .Dyfi memories. . . .no more goose shooting.

Sitting in the back of the car and clutching the map given to me by my geography teacher, it was early August and we were heading north along the West Wales coast road. To the left was the wide seascape of Cardigan Bay, and from the cliff-line that each year withstood Neptune's thunderous winter assault, the land climbed to the east through an unfolding patchwork of fields and wind-sculpted gorse clumps to the hazy high ground on the horizon. Beyond Aberaeron, with its small harbour littered with tired fishing boats lying on their sides in the mud, we came to the 'capital' of the coast, Aberystwyth. From here we cut inland, following the signposts to the town whose name is the bane of all non-Welsh speakers pronunciation, Machynlleth. Rounding a bend in the road before the reaching the village of Taliesin, named after the 6th century Welsh bardic equivalent of Chaucer, a wide vista opened before us.

To our left, shimmering in the summer heat haze lay the wide flat purple wetland of Cors Fochno, spangled with waving sedges and stunted alders and willows, leading the eye to the western horizon of the marram grass sand dunes of Borth. On our right the rolling hills climbed steadily to the Plynlimon moorlands, but straight ahead was the massive brooding presence of Cadaer Idris, mottled with the shadows of fleeting summer clouds and flanked with lesser hills which rose steep from sea level. At the foot of this massif, gleaming silver on a full tide, lay the estuary of the River Dyfi. Immediately my mind was captivated by the drama of the surroundings and my imagination ran wild with the thoughts of adventures to come. I was not alone in this feeling of excitement, sharing the back seat with me, Raymond's eyes were sparkling and John's comment 'Iesu, this looks good, man!' told of our anticipation. We drove down the track and parked beside the embankment where 'x' marked the spot on the map, and we tumbled out to explore our new surroundings. Immediately a pair of mallard quacked noisily off the reed-choked pond beside our car park, and we ran to the top of the bank to get our bearings, breathing in the tang of the saltmarsh air and peering through the heat haze. On our side of the bank the land stretched wild and flat towards Cors Fochno, on the other was a wide samphire and rush covered shelf which dropped off into the deep muddy and tidal channel of a stream that had been straightened to run directly down to a distant wooden railway bridge, and on into the estuary. On the far side of this channel there lay a wide expanse of intensively cultivated farmland, wrested from the sea in times past to produce its huge acreage of wheat, greens turning gold, rippling and swaying in the light summer breeze.

Sandwiches and drinks were consumed in haste on the crest of the bank before Jim and we three younger visitors set off towards the bridge, leaving mother behind to soak up the sun and bury herself in the latest Agatha Christie. High in the deep blue overhead a red kite, rare indeed in those days, caught a thermal on lazy wings and circled even higher before gilding inland to some remote wooded valley.

We reached the wooden bridge as the receding tide gurgled and swashed around the supports below. A redshank, disturbed by our sudden appearance flew off as it hurled melodious profanities in our direction, and the distant roar of surf on the estuary's offshore bar was occasionally punctuated by faint shouts and shrieks drifting down the wind from holiday-makers of Borth beach. The railway line sat atop its embankment, which also served as the sea wall that separated dry land from the salt marsh. On the estuary side, the ebb gradually revealed a wide band of samphire and purslane saltmarsh, which dropped down to spartina beds, which in turn slowly gave way to extensive glistening wet mudflats before reaching the main river channel on the far side of the estuary. Eight square miles of prime wildfowl habitat and at least three times the area of our marsh at Laughrne Ferry, we all immediately fell under the spell of this enchanting place. During the drive home it was unanimously agreed that this would be the venue of our annual 'opening day' camp.

We returned to the same car park late in the afternoon of August 30th. Pitching tent, unrolling bedding, with the three lads puffing vigorously to inflate airbeds while the two 'elders' sorted and stored food, connected the gas burners and cleared a space for an open camp fire, creating a circle of stones to form the hearth. The task of collecting driftwood from the tideline would fall to us juniors when we went exploring later. With muted excitement the guns and cartridges were checked for the umpteenth time, and we were each allocated a space inside the tent for our wildfowling kit so that coats, bags, boots, and other necessities were piled within easy reach of our beds.

The 'foraging' walk down to the bridge, armed with an assortment of binoculars, took place as the westering sun dipped closer to the horizon, bathing the glistening mudflats in a veneer of orange and red. We could hear mallard, the sound of females quacking loudly drifted to us from several directions, the raucous laugh of shelduck came from the tideway, and curlew were in abundance, their mournful and far-carrying calls the very essence of this margin between land and sea. That night as we sat round the camp fire, we heard the frequent whicker of wings and the creaking quack of mallard drakes as they left the saltings to feed on the arable land, now an extensive area of stubble after the wheat harvest.

We explored further on the following day, walking some distance along the railway line, searching the estuary through binoculars, trying to pick out any flight lines each time we saw duck in the air, and rushing down the embankment each time a train approached! Spreading out onto the saltings approximately where the second cross appeared on the map, each chose a spot for concealment. By gathering together tideline debris and other materials close at hand, hides were made in readiness for the following dawn, and the correct stepping-off point from the embankment marked with a conspicuous driftwood branch. On opening day, high tide would be around noon so we had the chance of three flights – dawn, dusk, and the mid-day tide flight. We decided to return to camp only when hunger drove us back! Again that night, against a background of glittering stars in a clear sky, we tracked the movements of

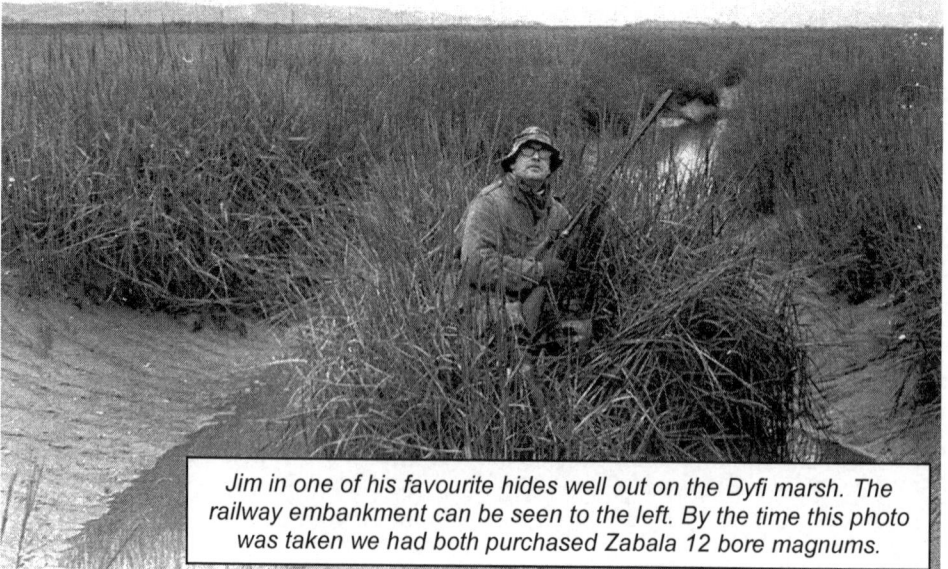

Jim in one of his favourite hides well out on the Dyfi marsh. The railway embankment can be seen to the left. By the time this photo was taken we had both purchased Zabala 12 bore magnums.

mallard flying over our encampment and guessed that the main direction of the morning flight would be from the stubble fields back onto the marsh. From that direction, they would be outlined against the lightening eastern horizon as dawn approached.

We were in our respective hides well before the eastern sky bore the first streaks of a late summer dawn. On our walk out, occasionally slipping and stumbling on awkwardly-spaced railway sleepers in the pre-dawn dark, we were serenaded by all manner of wader calls far out on the mud and the tide's edge, by occasional mallard voices from inland, all against a distant background rumble of surf from the offshore bar. I settled in to my little hole on the saltings, plastic sheet to sit on and an ex-army canvas bag wedged between the vegetation on the lip of the hide. In the light of the slowly fading stars two 'Alphamax' 16 bore cartridges rested in a fold in the canvas, the long brass head of each case gleaming softly, and beside the bag the loaded gun was ready for action. Ghostly shapes wafted overhead flying vague and erratic courses, seagulls heading inland. A lapwing, pinion feathers rattling with each down-stroke of its

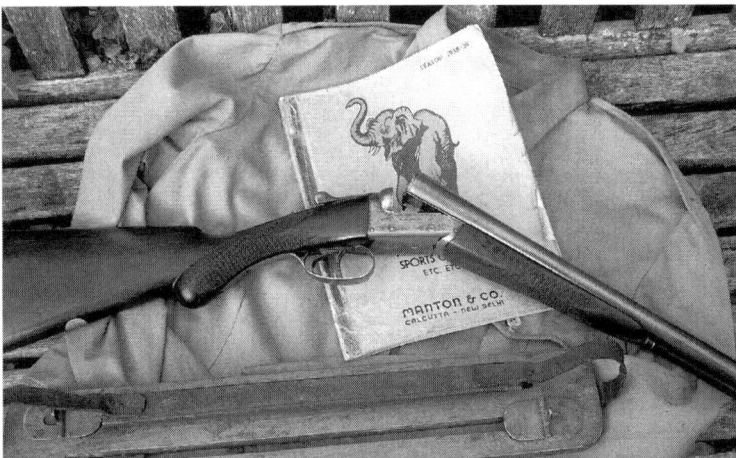

I took over the family's 16 bore Webley & Scott, originally bought for my mother from Manton's, Calcutta

wings, flashed past barely inches above my head when I heard the creaking of a mallard drake and a gunshot from further down the saltings. This was followed by dimly-seen shape emerging from the marsh and the sound of footfalls sloshing across the spartina-covered mud – Raymond had a bird down and was in hot pursuit. More shots as he disappeared back into concealment as both Jim and John had birds over them. A curlew came past my position, making for the fields for its breakfast and I followed its clear silhouette into the yellowing sky when it seemed to become split into two dots. With a start I realised the second dot was coming my way and I only had time to hurriedly throw the gun to my shoulder before the duck faded into the still-darkened sky overhead. At the sound of a splashy impact on the mud behind me, the only indication that my shot had connected, I was up and out of my hole and slogging across the marsh to where a dark blob lay on a bare mud-bank. My first duck from the Dyfi estuary. Some time later we heard a distant double gunshot and we assumed that somewhere between the camp and the bridge, Mother was wielding the 20 bore!

The sun was well up by the time hunger called us back to camp. At the driftwood marker on the railway embankment we gathered together to compare notes and birds. We had all noticed that as the duck flight ended, so the pigeon flight began. There appeared to be steady stream of pigeons crossing from the wooded hills on the north bank of the estuary to the corn stubbles beyond the sea wall on the south shore, so the other three delayed breakfast for a spot of pigeon flighting. I sat at the foot of the embankment to watch as I did not wish to use my precious heavy cartridges on pigeon. Only three weeks before I had visited the gunshop in Llandysul and asked if he stocked any Eley heavy-load 16 bore Alphamax or Hymax cartridges. Although he had not previously held this ammunition, he had just placed a cartridge order from the manufacturers in

Birmingham, and to my delight, Jack immediately picked up the phone and asked for 250 of each to be added to his order – I left the shop feeling very important!

Mother had seen us as we left the railway bridge to walk back up along the creek to our camp, and as we approached, carrying six mallard and the same number of pigeons, the smell of frying bacon hastened our final steps. Laid neatly beside the 20 bore was a fine drake teal in full winter plumage – we were correct in our surmise that my mother had been in action!

By late morning, after dozing fitfully for an hour or two in the warm September sunshine we made ready for the tide flight, and this time I added a handful of pigeon cartridges to one of my coat pockets. Just as we were about to leave, Dai's car drew up and he duly inspected his sons' morning bag with his customary comment of approval, 'Oh, very good!' With him came Geraint, the youngest of the three brothers and not committed to shooting. He was, nevertheless, a budding angler and had brought along his rod. We all set out again for the foreshore, suggesting to Geraint that he cast a speculative line into the creek as it filled by the rising tide, and left him and his father sitting on the flood bank as we turned onto the railway line. Discussing Geraint's chances of success, we concluded they were zero. For a start we had no knowledge of the presence of any fish in the estuary, and his tackle comprised a tiny kiddie's spinning rod, a mackerel spinner and some weights, and a decrepit reel holding ancient nylon line which bore knots all along its length!

The high tide came and went, and although a few duck were seen in the distance, only three pigeons were brought to bag. We were greeted on our return to the bridge by a jubilant youngest son, jumping with excitement, holding his fishing rod in one hand, and to our stunned amazement, an enormous plaice of over 2 ½ lbs in the other!

We broke camp after the dawn flight on the following morning, and tired, muddy, and happy, we turned south for home with ten mallard, two teal, three curlew, and a dozen pigeons in the boot of the car. This was the first of many expeditions to this magical place, and it was to be the venue for our September camps for the next five years. In reality, the opening day camps had become a ritual to celebrate the start of a new season. Sitting in the warm late-summer sunshine with the mud around your hide bubbling and hissing as the rising sun warmed its surface, and the sounds of holidaymakers drifting across the estuary from the sea strand, this was wildfowl shooting in non-wildfowling conditions. Even then, we came to the conclusion that true wildfowling only began when the bubble and whistle of wigeon announced their arrival, borne on the cold winds out of the north as the world closed down for winter. Then, perchance, we would also come into contact with the geese. My game book records the extreme contrasts we experienced in a sortie to the Dyfi two seasons later. The week before it had snowed quite heavily,- enough to cancel all the school buses though the school remained open. It was an adventure to walk the three miles to Llandysul along roads that only saw the occasional intrepid Royal Mail van clanking along on its tyre chains. With barely one third of the school's normal population in attendance, a carnival atmosphere reigned with ad-hoc mixed-age lessons, film shows, and concerts. Late in the week a partial thaw set in and the roads were cleared,- school reverted to normal. However, reports from further north told of severe sub-zero temperatures and although Raymond and John were unavailable, Jim and I quickly planned a wildfowling expedition to the Dyfi estuary for the Saturday.

We left the house at midnight on the Friday. At first we made good time as the roads were reasonably clear, but north of Aberaeron conditions became increasingly tricky. Several slides and a near-piling-the-car-into-a-hedge incident made progress more circumspect. Nearly six hours from setting out we parked up on the track leading to the saltings,- there was no time to lose if we were to be in position at dawn as we still had a two-mile walk ahead of us.

The freezing air hit us with a shock as we opened the car doors, but pullovers, coats and waders were quickly struggled on, cartridges stuffed into pockets and guns un-shipped as Jim slung the food and thermos haversack over his shoulder. We set out to walk the straight track along the deep canal to the railway bridge on the sea wall, and within a few yards my breath was already freezing on my balaclava.

In complete and silent darkness we climbed the embankment to the railway line and stood for a moment to regain our breath and to take stock of our surroundings. Across the estuary the street lights of Aberdovey twinkled in the brittle cold, the distant roar of surf on the bar at the estuary's mouth was interrupted by the occasional melancholy wail of a lapwing or the haunting cry of a curlew, far out on the mudflats. We turned to walk along the railway embankment to reach our chosen saltings, stopping frequently when we heard the sleepy gabbling of white-fronted geese on the estuary or the whistle and churr of wigeon over the huge stubble fields on the inland side of the track. In the intense darkness that precedes dawn, there was one noise that was new to us. For a young teenager with a vivid imagination it was scary. From far out across the mudflats there came a deep and unearthly groaning, interspersed with crashing and splintering noises. 'Jim, what the hell was that?' I squeaked, only to be told 'Shut up and keep walking!' - it was evident that he didn't know either! We left the embankment and cut out onto the saltings, crossing some short-cropped salt pasture before reaching the spartina. The recent tideline was marked by an enormous jumble of sheets and blocks of ice, piled on the edge of the spartina like a line of bulldozed rubble. At last, just as the eastern stars were beginning to fade we reached our favourite hides beside a deep creek and settled in for the coming of dawn.

As I checked my barrels and loaded my 16 bore with a couple of 'Alphamax 4's' I swivelled around in my muddy hide to face the railway embankment, peering through the sharp-edged and frosted spartina towards the lightening

Looking through, and not over the sharp-edged spartina on the Dyfi estuary

eastern skyline. We were after wigeon coming back to the estuary from their night foraging on the inland stubbles. Several times during our walk out, packs had passed over our heads, bubbling and whistling to each other in the icy darkness, and our hopes were running high for a good flight

The north wind, blowing down from the snow-locked peak of Cadaer Idris which sat brooding over the north shore of the estuary, was beginning to seep through my clothing now that I had begun to cool down from the recent forced march. The low hills of the eastern horizon were now black against the vivid yellow of the sky, when a ragged party of teal swept past me too suddenly for me to react, and only then did I discover that the fingertips of my right hand were frozen to the gun barrels. For several precious minutes I tried breathing on them in an effort to release them, but this seemed only to make matters worse! In desperation I called to Jim and a small quantity of warm coffee poured onto the barrels quickly brought relief just as a big pack of wigeon roared overhead.

For the next hour, we both experienced the flight of a lifetime. We could hear the duck coming while they were still some distance away and invisible against the dark background of the hills. Suddenly they would appear as they crossed the horizon into the pale dawn sky, fleeting and weaving black silhouettes which faded from view as they flew across the still darkened sky overhead. All thoughts of frozen gun barrels were forgotten in the quick dashes out of the hide to retrieve downed birds, and by the end of that time six wigeon lay in the spartina beside a small pile of empty cartridges. I stopped shooting,- six birds was all I could carry comfortably and I made this my self-imposed limit. Jim fired two more cartridges which also brought his tally to six, though his bag included two mallard. I stumbled over to his hide to open the flask of soup, and we sat together as small parties of wigeon and teal continued to flight from inland. We could easily have shot a dozen birds each, but were content to watch the pageant of dawn unfold around us on this wild estuary.

Somewhere far out on the sands the geese began to stir themselves, talking more urgently to each other until the moment's silence before they all took wing,- a wavering line above the sand dunes of Borth some miles down the estuary. It was now light enough to see clearly and the source of the unearthly night-time noises revealed itself. Beyond the exposed mudflats, the main river channel was a swirl of large ice floes moving down to meet the now rising tide. Thick blocks colliding with each other and being up-ended by the maelstrom of currents and eddies produced the whole range of noises we heard in the darkness. The oncoming tide began to spread across the mud, lifting the thin ice sheets that had formed since the last tide, and all the waders on the estuary heralded the rising water and new day in a truly wild chorus.

Suddenly Cadaer Idris was lost from view as a yellow-grey curtain approached from the north and the bright morning light faded. It was 9 o'clock and despite many layers of clothing, I was beginning to shiver uncontrollably as the snowstorm hit us. Visibility was reduced to a few yards as we packed up and threaded our way along the quietly filling creek to the safety of the railway embankment, and thence back to the car. With the heater turned to full we gradually thawed out as we made the slow journey homeward, and with this thaw came excruciating pain from the frost marks and blisters on my fingertips!

I have never experienced such intense cold in the years of winter wildfowling adventures since that morning flight. It could be that when we have been hit by cold weather I have 'gone soft' and had the sense to stay indoors, but I rather think that we just have not had true winter conditions for a number of years.

Another day, another dawn. Several times we had tried to get under the geese, turning left from the railway bridge towards the west and the sea, rather than going upstream as we usually did for the duck. Each time, whether for their morning flight when they left the estuary for a day's grazing on Cors Fochno, or in the evening when they returned at the very edge of darkness, they crossed the embankment just tantalisingly out of our of reach. Leaving home in the small hours in order to be in position by first light, the final leg of the journey was very slow as we were driving through thick fog. In pitch darkness we felt our way along the shelf down to the bridge, and with many a stumble and curse turned west along the railway track towards Ynyslas. Fearing to use a torch, I soon gave up this line and slid down the bank, through the fence and onto the saltings.   Jim pressed on and left me to fumble across the salt pasture until I found a reasonably dry hole to fall into. The sound of Jim's footsteps quickly died away as I tried to make myself comfortable while cradling the gun. It was an eerie environment. For the first

Whitefronts, well out of range, head out to Cors Fochno from the estuary on a sunny morning

time in all our visits I could not hear the surf, and even the occasional calls of wildfowl and wader seemed muted and strangled by the enshrouding fog. In the murk I could see no boundary between ground and sky and this did not improve as almost imperceptibly, my surroundings changed from black to charcoal, and finally to a dull grey. Every now and then the fog lifted slightly and barely forty yards away I glimpsed the nearest telegraph pole on the embankment. I reached for a driftwood stick and laid it on the lip of my hole, pointing it in the direction of safety should the fog thicken again. A small party of wigeon passed low over my head somewhere in gloom. I did not catch sight of them but I would have held my fire anyway, we were waiting for geese. Checking my watch it was well past 8.00am, and somewhere up there it was broad daylight. Perhaps the geese had decided not to move, I mused to myself, when suddenly they broke out into a chorus of high-pitched chatter. They were in the air! I gripped the stock harder and peered into the fog, it was too late now to check if the gun was loaded! Straining both eyes and ears, it was not long before I realised, with sinking despair, that they would pass well to my right . As Jim was somewhere to my left, yet again they had beaten our attempts at interception. I waited for another twenty minutes and then slowly and with stiff limbs I stood to gather my kit and return to the sea wall I could now see vaguely through the swirling white tendrils. Unloading the gun, I stooped to pick up my bag when a single goose call came from the landward side. Feverishly struggling to pull two cartridges from my pocket with a gloved hand, I only had time to hurriedly push one into the right barrel before a single goose, still calling loudly, appeared almost overhead. Shooting by pure instinct, to my absolute delight the bird folded in mid-air and bounced onto the soft rush at the edge of the saltings. My joyous shrieks reached Jim, and he came hurrying along the line to pump my hand enthusiastically in his congratulations! I was thirteen years old and it was my first, and as it turned out, my only white-fronted goose from the Dyfi estuary.

We had read about punt-gunning. James Wentworth-Day's exploits with silent punts and mighty guns grabbed our imagination, and pooling our resources with a little maternal financial backing, we bought a two-seater fibreglass canoe. It was quite unlike the dart-shaped vessels one sees today, and it compared favourably with the form and line of a full-decked Payne-Gallwey gunning punt. What was even more surprising was its stability –we never actually managed to capsize it despite making deliberate attempts to do so. We also bought some lobster creels and spent one summer holiday based in our caravan in Cei Bach, catching lobsters to cook and sell to passing holidaymakers on the beach. Over the course of that summer we made around £200 from this trade, which amply paid for the canoe, repaid various parental loans and gave us cartridge money for the year. By the autumn, its sky-blue deck and white hull and been repainted battleship grey, and it was launched into the creek leading to the bridge as the spring tide was filling.

Lacking a punt gun to mount on its bows, Jim's Greener GP, loaded with an optimistic 1¼ oz of BB shot would have to do. My 16 bore was to be the 'cripple-stopper'. So we set off, under the bridge and out onto the wide expanse of water on the estuary. Working upstream along the margin of the marsh, paddling in deep water and poling over the mud, we 'set to' many groups of 'fowl, but unlike many of the accounts we had read, the duck saw our approach and either swam contemptuously away or lifted off only to re-settle a few hundred yards further on. The tide had reached its peak, and soon I noticed the flotsam and bubbles start to move ominously back towards the sea. Gone were the visions of a big flock shot, as no duck had allowed us to approach to within one hundred yards.

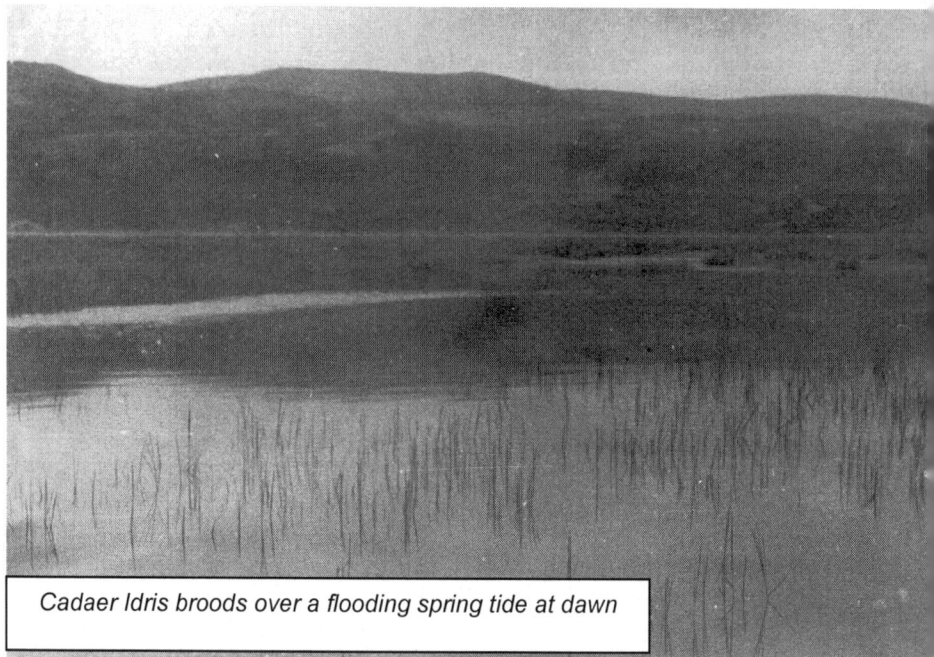

Cadaer Idris broods over a flooding spring tide at dawn

Rounding a small spartina headland we came across an unsuspecting curlew and this was the only victim of our 'punt-gunning' expedition. While the bird was being retrieved, the canoe grounded on a mud-bank and there followed a frantic search for a deep water creek that would lead us back towards the bridge. My memory still recoils from the gruelling return to the car. Battling against the currents in a rapidly draining estuary, dragging the vessel across soft mud, and the slow and arduous progress upstream from the bridge. Sitting mud be-smeared and exhausted in the car, Jim and I decided that it had been a very silly idea and that we would forever after remain shore-shooters!

Sitting at my keyboard and with frequent references to the old game book lying open on my desk, I have been astonished by the number of images and memories that I thought were long-forgotten but, like the tide, have come gently and silently flooding back.

Tucked in between the boulders flanking the railway embankment late into the night, with Cadaer Idris wearing its gleaming white winter shroud in the moonlight, and the rush, bubbling and whistle of wigeon packs around us. Sudden snap shots at fleeting blurred shapes against the background of high stratus clouds, and the crackling impact of a downed bird as it broke through the hoar-frosted vegetation in its fall.

Of the high spring tide that covered the track to a depth of a few inches. Paddling back through this to the car park on a dark moonless night, where every splashing step produced a wonderful cascading firework display of green phosphorescence.

The hair-raising journey back from the Dyfi in a dreadfully over-laden little blue 1938 Austin Seven, it was Raymond's first car and he was an unqualified driver. Avoiding main roads wherever possible, at every bump and pot-hole the rear wheels hit the wheel arches and each time this happened we left little blue-grey puffs of burnt rubber smoke in our wake.

Of the still and clear night when the black and brooding mass of Cadaer Idris was back-lit by blues and greens of Nature's own celestial firework display, the Aurora Borealis.

The time when staying out in the hide for 'just a few minutes more' haunted my nightmares for months. Silent and deadly, the rising tide had filled the creek behind me and in the deepening February twilight I went up to my neck in swirling tide-driven water with soft mud ever sucking at my boots before, soaked through and very frightened, I reached safe ground.

The fiery red sunsets over the sea and the yellow gash of dawn over the eastern hills, and always, the smell of the mudflats and the wild chorus of myriad waders and wildfowl from the tideline - the choral symphony of the marsh, clear and melodious above the insistent bass-rhythm of distant pounding surf.

The Dyfi estuary had given me a decade of wildfowling, and in that time the over-wintering geese had dwindled from around four hundred to less than one hundred. Long before this low point had been reached I made the decision to stop shooting grey geese. Inevitably, on three occasions after coming to this conclusion I had a skein of whitefronts right overhead within easy range, but I held to my decision. After all, in my brief wildfowling lifetime they had abandoned Carmarthen Bay, both drainage and land reclamation had driven them away from Arthur Cadman's favourite venue on the wide inland bog of Cors Tregaron in the upper Teifi valley. Now their presence on this wild and magical estuary was in jeopardy, and I did not wish to bear partial responsibility for such a tragic loss.

At the age of twenty-two I left Wales to take up a teaching post in Reading. My life was about to change and I was not to return to the Dyfi estuary for the next twenty years.

At 17, with a drake wigeon and a new Zabala 12 magnum

Part 2. Intermission

Chapter 5: THE MOVE INLAND

End of college and the big wide world, , ,.Reading. . . . .work and marriage. . . Thames-side horror,- .renounce shooting?. . . . .gun in storage in Wales. . . .discovering the Wildfowl Trust,- Slimbridge, and Welney. . . .wildfowl photography. . . .a promotion.

The carefree years of college education was a time spent playing much sport, partying, drinking silly quantities of weak beer, and although regularly interrupted by such trivialities as lectures and the occasional teaching practice, generally having a good time. This period ended with the bump of my coming back down to earth. During my college days my parents' divorce was finalised and Penyrallt was sold, and the new Firearms Act dispensed with the Post Office gun licence in favour of the new police-issued Shotgun Certificate. Thus, as Mother had left Wales for the ex-pat community in Spain, on leaving college I was of 'no fixed abode', which meant that I could no longer legally own a shotgun. I gave my Zabala 12 bore magnum into John's safe keeping while I struck out into the big wide world.

Barely three days before schools were due to begin a new September term, I was urgently summoned to a school in Reading for an interview. I was greeted by the Deputy Head with the words, 'Ah, you must be Mr Marshall-Ball, here's the timetable you are going to teach, the term begins on Monday'. It was late on Friday afternoon and I wasn't even shown round the school. So much for a formal interview, I had forty-eight hours to find accommodation, settle in my meagre belongings , and try to prepare a scheme of work for the coming week! My official title was 'Assistant Teacher of Geography' in an establishment which was totally different to my own experience of schooling - an urban Bilateral School for Boys. In those days, a bilateral school housed 'grammar school' pupils (those that had passed the 11+ examination), and 'secondary' pupils (the 11+ failures) on the same site, and in this school's case, in the same building. The shock of teaching 'A' level geography in one lesson and facing a class of fourteen-year-old non-readers in the next required a very steep learning curve for any greenhorn teacher to survive in the blackboard jungle.

From the start, it was an existence of total commitment. Coaching school sports teams after school, lesson preparation and marking on weekday evenings, coaching or refereeing school rugby matches on Saturdays, and recuperating after playing rugby for a local club on Sundays. Despite having so little time to myself, the pressure of this new way of life suited me and I enjoyed my time in Reading. Even during the holidays, field trips, holiday camps, and sports tours bit a sizeable chunk out of vacation periods, and it was always expected that the junior teachers should contribute most to these activities. With no home to go back to in Wales, any thoughts of shooting in my spare time had sunk well below the horizon.

Also during this maelstrom existence I met Shelagh, a student at the local Teacher Training College, and after a whirlwind romance of barely four months, she became my bride. By now I had been promoted to 2nd in charge of the Geography Department and I cut down on some of my sporting commitments to the school as I settled down to married life. As to my past, I had casually remarked that I had grown up with guns and fishing, but although she accepted the angling, she had a suspicion of guns in general and I don't think she wanted to dwell on the shooting aspect of my growing up,. At the time she was not very knowledgeable about wildlife matters, but she nevertheless loved the countryside, so on summer evenings and weekends we would spend hours in the local wildlife park near Wallingford, and take long walks along the Thames. It was on one such occasion when a small trip of mallard flew overhead and I mounted an imaginary gun to take a left and right. I was stunned by the horrified look in my new wife's face. 'How can you even pretend' she said with tears brimming her eyes, 'to kill such beautiful birds?'

I needed to do some serious thinking, but for the time being my gun remained 'in storage' with John in Wales, and the topic of shooting was dropped from conversation.

We discovered the Wildfowl Trust. Many weekends we would escape from Reading to Slimbridge, where we would bed-and-breakfast at 'The Patch' and spend all hours of daylight wandering the grounds, ensconced in a hide overlooking 'The Dumbles' salt marsh watching through binoculars the comings-and-goings of white-fronted geese, the large resident flock of barnacle geese, and the activity of all manner of wildfowl. As darkness fell we would retire to the heated observation room called the 'Swan Observatory' to watch the Bewicks and Whoopers arrive for their evening meal. Here at least, among the many exotic species that added their own calls to the cacophony at feeding time, I was always straining to hear the calls of our own native wildfowl, the wigeon, teal, pintail that were drawn from the estuary to feed on the outer edge of the floodlit lake. Shelagh encouraged my photography, and over the years I acquired a number of long lenses for my ancient Russian Zenith camera, and a complete darkroom set including enlarger, developing trays, and various noxious chemicals in order to pursue the hobby.

We ventured further afield to Welney in Lincolnshire. During each visit I was stunned by the sight of several thousand wigeon during each evening flight, more duck than I had ever seen in my wildfowling days on the Point or on the Dyfi, and though I had become a non-shooter, the call of wildfowl still stirred my blood. These visits were followed by us both spending hours in our bathroom, which had been converted into a makeshift darkroom, in order to produce a whole library of monochrome images of wildfowl on the Welney Washes. However, sitting in a heated observation hide and watching the pageant of Bewick's swans and all manner of wildfowl going about their daily activities on the wide sheet of wash flood-water just did not feel the same as being out on the saltings with gun in hand at dawn. Even so and despite my misgivings, I made up my mind to renounce shooting and to concentrate, using the primitive equipment which was all we could afford, on wildfowl photography.

I spent four years teaching in the bilateral school in Reading before I was appointed to the post of Head of Geography in a little rural comprehensive school in Lincolnshire. In all this time I had not handled, let alone fired, any firearm. Shortly before we moved north I telephoned John with the request to sell my gun. His reply was blunt, 'Don't be so bloody stupid, Rob! I refuse to sell your gun. . .you've always been a shooter and sooner or later you'll come back to it. Your gun's here until you are ready!'. With that he put the phone down!

House hunting for properties within our limited price range took us to some remote locations in this area which combined intensive arable farming and heavy urban industry. Within a radius of twenty miles from my new school there were many houses to see, and as all house-hunters do, each property was discussed and analysed at length. There was one we both liked, a solid inter-war semi-detached house with a nice garden, but our only reservation was that there was a large industrial works three fields away from the front of the house which really spoiled the view from the front room. We returned to our flat in Reading only to hear the breaking news that the house we had just recently visited had been completely demolished in a huge industrial explosion – the property was on the edge of a village called Flixborough.

We eventually bought a house at the foot of virtually the only slope in north Lincolnshire and within a mile of the school on the fringe of Kirton in Lindsey, a settlement described in a Shell Guide book as 'a decaying old market town gently sliding down the hillside'. We quickly settled in to our first house, bringing with us three muscovy ducks which we named 'Jemima Puddle-duck',' 'Christmas Dinner', and 'New-Year's Dinner', just to keep them guessing! To this trio and after I had excavated and lined a pond in our large garden, we added two Canada geese, a barnacle goose inevitably called 'William' from a local wildfowl collection, and a drake mallard called 'Robert' after the pupil who had brought the tiny duckling into school.

When we arrived, shooting of any sort was far from my mind as we settled happily into our new home, but within a year I was grateful that John had so stubbornly refused my telephoned request.

Chapter 6. THE MOVE NORTH

. . . wide skies and open landscape. . . . ..rural school. . . .invitation to shoot. . . . .recall gun. . . rough shooting. . . ..a magnum for driven partridge?. . . . .teaching others. . . . .a course for students. . . .a failed writer. . . . .Tony and Arthur. . . . .Gainsborough Wildfowlers. . . .the move south.

For someone growing up in the rounded and wooded hilly landscape of the Teifi valley where the horizon was seldom more than a mile or two away, north Lincolnshire was an alien environment. My own classroom, inevitably on the top floor of the school's tower block (as geography rooms seem to be in every school I have seen) gave me a vista across the Ancholme valley to the low rolling horizon of the Lincolnshire Wolds beyond Caistor to the east. On a clear day I could see forty miles in this direction, and from the edge of the town the view westwards took in the series of power station cooling towers along the Trent, receding southwards into the dim distance.

Here was a part of England that I quickly grew to realise had a character and charm of its own. Moving from the rolling hills of west Wales and claustrophobia of urban Reading, the wide and un-cluttered horizons gave a profound feeling of space and freedom, and the huge skies provided a never-ending pageant of tumbling cloudscapes, with clear skies sparkling blue in the sharp frosts of winter and shimmering in the heat of summer sun. Every night, from our house we could watch a spectacular display when the northern sky glowed orange and red above the blast furnaces of the Scunthorpe's steel works a dozen miles away, giving true credence to the industrial town's motto 'The Heavens reflect our Labours'.

My new school, a little rural comprehensive with eighteen staff and just over four hundred pupils, was much more to my liking, and much more like the schools I had attended in Wales. After the initial stressful time when a teacher needs to establish his or herself within a new school, I began to enjoy my new job and the countryside around our new home. Some time during the first term I was walking round my class of fourteen-year-olds when I overheard two boys having a whispered conversation about their weekend shooting. My ears pricked up, and rather than tell them off for not concentrating on the task in hand, I surreptitiously edged closer to eavesdrop more clearly!

At the end of the lesson I called them back and began my interrogation. After advising them that I had very good hearing and that they had been remiss at not carrying out the task in hand, I said, 'Now, what's all this about shooting?'. . . .No answer for some time, then with eyes cast down a muttered comment, 'Teachers don't like us talking about shooting, sir, they say it's cruel'. My next question, 'Were you shooting or beating?'. 'Beating for most of the day, but our dad let me have a shot on the last walk'. 'Oh,' I replied, 'what sort of gun?'

'It's a shotgun, sir, you know, one that fires loads of little lead pellets. My dad has a 20 bore he lets me use.' They were taken aback by my next comment, 'I hope you don't mix up your cartridges with 12 bores'. It suddenly struck them that this was not the usual way a conversation about shooting went with a teacher. Their faces brightened, 'Hey-up, sir, do you shoot?'

Within a matter of hours word had got round the school, and on playground duties thereafter I often acquired a posse of boys, and a few girls, anxious to tell me their tales of beating, shooting, and inevitably some of surreptitious poaching adventures that a teacher really should not hear. Despite images of my own childhood adventures flashing into my mind, nevertheless I think I put on a convincing display of teacherly disapproval for the young and keen audience.

'Parents Evening' near the end of the spring term, and before me sat 'Baz' Glover whose son I taught. Nearing the end of the customary and routine conversation of the boy's classroom performance, he interrupted me with the words, 'Now then! Let's get down to important things! . . . .I have heard that you're a shooting man, so I'm going to fix up some dates for you to come out with us next season'. With mounting and barely suppressed excitement I begged more details. 'It's just a rough shoot, like, - me and the lads have a walk around for partridge and pheasant, with the odd hare thrown in and some duck from the ponds.' I told him where my gun was, 'You'd better send for it then!', was the comment as he departed and the next parent was ushered in. This conversation had the same effect on my concentration as the time, many years before, when my geography teacher had shown me the map of the Dyfi estuary and uttered the magic word, 'geese'. The remainder of the evening passed in blurred haze of excitement which bore no relation to the prospect of meeting so many parents for the first time.

Shelagh was not impressed, but to her credit she accepted the inevitable on the basis that it could be seen as one way of integrating with the local community and interacting with parents of the pupils I taught. I needed a shotgun certificate, and when the form had been duly completed and countersigned by one of my fellow teachers from Reading, I received the customary visit from the local constable. What was intended to be a brief visit to check my suitability for possessing a shotgun, it lasted much longer as we talked for hours about our respective shooting experiences, and he left with the accurate forecast that we would meet again in the field. Two weeks later, the brown envelope marked 'Humberside Constabulary' dropped through our letterbox and once again I became a legal gun owner.

I phoned John, 'It's about bloody time! Your gun hasn't been fired for five years,. . .are you doing anything next weekend?', he asked. 'Good! I don't trust the Post Office so I'll bring it up to you!'

In early October I had a call to meet them on the following Saturday. Rough shooting with Baz was a new experience as I had not shot in a group this large before. We usually gathered in a lay-by north of Kirton, where I first met the motley crew that made up his syndicate. Even after three years of shooting in their company, with the exception of Baz, I never got to know their real names. There was Mo, Ed, Stitch, and a number of other regulars, all dressed in rough old weather-beaten jackets, usually tied round the waist with string or a battered old cartridge belt, patchy corduroy trousers, and industrial boots. More than anything, it was also a social gathering of old and trusted friends whom I quickly realised were also careful and safe gun handlers and good shots. Laughter and ribaldry ruled the day, yet we also managed to flush and shoot a respectable number of birds. The shooting day was organised on a 'walk and stand' basis. One or two Guns would be sent forward and we would walk the ground towards them. The main venue was the derelict limestone quarry and adjacent land, but at other times we would shoot over farmland at Cleatham and on the disused Blyton airfield.

My first outing was a complete disaster and I ended the day convinced that I would never be invited out again. I was introduced with the words, 'This is Robin, the new teacher at the big school', and the motley crew eyed both me and the Zabala magnum I was carrying with equal suspicion. In my defence I had not fired a shotgun at a live target in six years, my experience of pheasants was extremely limited, and for partridge it was non-existent. Compared to my memories of 'walkabout' rough shooting with Raymond and John in Wales, the amount of game on Baz Glover's rough shoot was a revelation! Every stubble field or patch of rough ground held a covey or two of either grey or red-legged partridge, and pheasants popped up from the most unlikely and un-promising locations. They did not breed and release any birds on their ground, and we were taking a harvest from purely wild-bred game. My game book records eleven cartridges fired during the course of the day and I had not touched a feather! Although all my new acquaintances were encouraging and supportive, I felt a total fraud! I apologised to Baz at the end of the day, reluctantly but gratefully accepting the brace of pheasants he handed to me, after all, I explained, I had contributed nothing to the bag. Gently he took me aside, 'The lads want to know if you'd like to come with us in two week's time, when we're shooting Cleatham'. I was both amazed and very relieved and asked, judging by my performance today, if they were really serious. 'Look', he said in his broad Lincolnshire accent while laying a reassuring hand on my shoulder, 'we can tell you're not a beginner, and we've seen you're a safe shot, so you've just had an off day. It's hardly surprising as you 'ent shot for so many years'. As the others were departing, many bade me farewell with a friendly smile and the words, '. . .see you in a fortnight!'

Proudly I entered the house and tried to hand my two prized pheasants to my wife for processing. I immediately realised that this was a big mistake, as through much squealing and gesticulation I was given to understand that if I must bring these birds home, she would have no truck with them. Her interest would only be aroused when they were cooked and served up on the dinner table! This was not the way I had become used to. During all my previous shooting exploits I had simply handed the quarry over to my mother, and although I was adept at plucking, I had no experience of drawing and trussing to produce 'oven ready' birds! Mrs Beaton's book was consulted and the photo sequence for preparing a chicken was carefully followed. Although there were occasional squeamish moments, I completed the task and presented the two carcasses to my wife, who was now rather more prepared to look at them as they bore some resemblance at least, to a shop-bought chicken. I didn't mind. Since that day on the Thames riverbank when I had pretended to shoot at mallard, Shelagh had come a very long way to an acceptance of shooting as a means of bringing food to the table. We did agree, however, that I should take charge of cooking any birds, beasts, or fish I brought home.

Cleatham was much better. Pushed forward to be a standing gun on the second walk, three coveys of partridge were driven over me. When the walking guns approached at the end of the drive, although my heart was doing somersaults with excitement, I casually held up four birds for my six cartridges. Baz shook my hand, 'I knew it were only a matter of time. Lad!', and he quickly reorganised the walkers and standers for the next patch of rough ground. I ended the day with a tally of seven partridge and one pheasant at a cost of fourteen cartridges, and basked in the congratulatory comments from my new-found friends. I felt accepted as part of the group.

Glancing around the other members of Baz Glover's syndicate, there was a wider choice of weapon than I had ever seen before or since. Two sported ancient hammer guns, and although over and under shotguns were the most popular choice, there was a sprinkling of side-by-sides, one pump-action repeater, and a Browning 5-shot self-loader. I was beginning to feel that my tightly choked and heavy 12 bore magnum was quite inappropriate and I was 'over-gunned' for rough shooting. We walked long distances during the course of each shooting day and by the last drive the Zabala was beginning to feel decidedly cumbersome. The end-of-season hare shoot was the final decider. Showing my inexperience of this form of shooting, I found myself on one long walk heavily encumbered by my gun and three hares. Only then did I fully understand the awful consequences of the principle, 'He who shoots it, carries it!', and I soon learned to leave the hares to the standing guns! A short time later the magnum was sold to Graham Leonard's gunshop in Brigg, and I bought Mo's spare over and under, a primitive double-trigger non-ejector Russian Baikal which was to serve me well over the next decade. I took it to my local gunsmith, Rob Marper, to have it checked over. After his customary greeting of 'Now then!', he gave it his scrutiny and pronounced it fit for purpose. 'There's nowt wrong with Baikals', he declared in his slow drawl, 'I sold this gun to Mo some years ago and he's shot a lot with it. It's built like a tank and will last you a lifetime, but you'll have to replace the hinge pin now and again 'cos that's where they wear loose'. Over my time in Lincolnshire I spent many hours in the portacabin that served as his workshop, and it was there that I first handled a Purdey shotgun, a thumb-hole opening hammer gun. He also owned the first 8 bore I had ever seen, a great double hammer gun by William Moore & Grey, and hefting this gun to my shoulder re-kindled all the images of wildfowling described by Scott, Wentworth-Day, Savory, and Cadman. Although at the time I had given up thoughts of goose shooting, nevertheless I hoped that one day I would have an 8 bore of my own, just as a reminder of the golden age of wildfowling in the inter-war years. Little did I realise at the time how grey geese populations, and my own perceptions of wildfowling, would change.

One Monday morning I walked into my geography room to find a very subdued class of fifteen-year-old pupils. Instantly I knew something was badly wrong and in shocked tones one of the lads told the tale of the weekend. John, who should have been occupying the desk by the window in my classroom, had been out on a nefarious escapade with a shotgun on the Saturday evening. Having crawled through a hedge he had pulled the gun after him and it had 'gone off', removing most of his upper arm. I was both appalled and struck by an immense sense of guilt – I really felt that I could have done something to prevent this horrendous accident. That night Shelagh and I talked over the incident for hours and the result of much heart-searching was the ground plan for a course of instruction in shotgun safety.

On the following morning I discussed the idea with my headteacher, and although he held considerable reservations, in the light of John's accident he accepted it in principle as an after-school course. After all, according to my outline plan it would involve bringing shotguns onto school premises and he would only allow this if there was active police involvement and approval. By the weekend I had a promise of help from Graham Leonard from his Brigg gunshop, and I had contacted the Brigg station of Humberside Police. The Chief Inspector, himself a shotgun shooter, called at the school and in a meeting with the school's Head, we agreed on how the police should be involved. The Game Conservancy Trust made a number of 16mm films available, including a crucial film on safe gun

Graham Leonard coaches the pupils on my first safety course while Baz Glover (extreme right) looks on.

handling entitled 'Dead Safe', and the course was launched a few weeks later. Every Thursday evening for eight weeks there were film shows, talks by police officers who were themselves shooters, and demonstrations of various types of shotguns by Graham Leonard. On the Saturday following the final classroom element of the course, the first group met at the clay pigeon ground on the southern end of the local airfield to practice and demonstrate safe gun-handling skills in a live-firing session. Graham Leonard coached shooting safety, stance, and technique, while the Chief Inspector and some parents acted as his assistants. At the end of this activity the policeman approached me with the reassuring words, 'These lads will be OK, and you've done well!'

At the school assembly on the Monday morning he presented a 'Certificate in Shotgun Safety', signed on behalf of Humberside Police, to the participants. All my subsequent courses were quickly over-subscribed.

Girls were also keen to learn shooting. Jess Goodale, Angie Sergeant, and Toni Colbourne (back row) in the second group to undergo shotgun safety training

When I arrived in Kirton I began trying to write articles for shooting and countryside magazines, but I really came to see myself as a failed writer because over the space of two years I had accumulated a dossier of rejection slips and returned articles. Undaunted, I continued to burn the midnight oil over an ancient typewriter compiling articles on matters shooting and fishing, but still the editors spurned my efforts. Following the first run of my course I wrote an account of my school's shotgun safety programme for 'Shooting Magazine' and to my great joy, it was accepted for publication – at last, after so many rejections, I had a published article.

There were two consequences of this momentous achievement. I quickly re-submitted many articles that had previously been rejected, only to be informed that now they were accepted for publication – my attempts at freelance writing had finally borne fruit.

The second consequence is that I received a telephone call at school from John Anderton, the Director of WAGBI (Wildfowlers Association of Great Britain and Ireland), summoning me down to the Head Office near Wrexham. As anyone who ever met 'JA' would understand, refusing such a summons verged on the impossible, and a few weeks later I met with members of WAGBI's staff, Gerry Turner, John Richards, and their new recruit, John Swift, to describe how my course was organised and how it could be adapted for a wider clientele. In due course Gerry Turner launched WAGBI's 'National Shotgun Proficiency Award Scheme', which though considerably modified for a far wider audience, nevertheless contained the core of what had been included in the Huntcliff School's 'Certificate in Shotgun Safety'. Though in the intervening years WAGBI has changed to BASC (British Association for Shooting and Conservation) the Proficiency Award Scheme, with many revisions and modifications, continues to flourish as a guide for newcomers to shotgun shooting.

When my friend John had travelled up from south Wales to deliver my gun, he also brought my fly fishing tackle. Although the prospect of sea trout or salmon fishing was non-existent in this remote part of north Lincolnshire, I did have the opportunity of fly fishing for still-water trout close at hand. This was a new experience for me as I had never before fished for rainbow trout. Toft Newton was a large concrete bowl of a reservoir and required a fundamental change of technique and tactics. On the Teifi the ability and tackle to cast up to around fifteen yards was perfectly adequate for the river, but in this new environment I needed to put my fly much further out in order to reach fish. With my limited resources I re-equipped with weight-forward mill end fly lines with which my whippy fibreglass rods could extend my casting distance, and the first fish I brought home were far easier to prepare for cooking, and far more acceptable to my wife, than any game bird.

Arthur and Jean, friends from our time in Reading when Jean worked on the same office as Shelagh, came to visit us regularly. A coarse angler to the core, I took Arthur to Toft Newton one afternoon so he could try his hand at fly fishing. For someone who was used to sitting by the riverbank watching a float, Arthur took to the activity of fly fishing very well and soon learned the rudiments of casting. His first fish, a rainbow trout of around two pounds, took him completely by surprise and after it was netted he complained that it was much more lively than a roach, and due to his aching wrist, he could 'never play with himself again!'. Later, he would also succumb to the lure of shotgun shooting and we would spend many an enjoyable hour hovering over a simple clay pigeon trap in order to develop his hand-eye co-ordination so that he was breaking clay targets consistently. Some years later, after we had moved south from Lincolnshire it was on Arthur's insistence that I again renewed my acquaintance with the Dyfi estuary and my love of wildfowling was re-kindled.

Tony was the tractor driver on a farm in the nearby village of Grayingham. Though a countryman born and bred, he also had no experience of shotgun shooting. One day while rooting around in one of the farm's store-rooms he came upon a small clay pigeon trap. This discovery had a catalytic effect. Often I would arrive home from school to find an unsigned note pinned to our front door. . . . *'Don't mess about! Got box of clays and cartridges. Get here now!'* When Shelagh returned from work we would go over to Grayingham and while she and Marilyn pooled resources to produce an evening meal, Tony would be learning to shoot. It was only a matter of months before Marilyn secretly asked me to find a gun for him, and on his birthday, much to his delight he was presented with an AyA Yeoman side-by-side 12 bore.

His first live quarry experience came on farmland adjoining the straightened River Ancholme at Brandy Wharfe. Will Wells, the farmer and parent of one of my pupils, was holding an end of season 'walkabout'. I gladly accepted his invitation and he asked me to bring one other to make up numbers. The day was memorable for a number of reasons. High winds and almost horizontal rain storms, meeting a pike angler with two enormous pike on the riverbank – I found it hard to believe such large predatory fish could have come from such a small and insignificant waterway, and Tony's first partridge, taken from a covey that burst into the air from his feet. However, the most memorable feat of the day came from our host. Will had given his 12 bore to his son for the day as a reward for completing my shotgun safety course in school, so he was left with a three-shot bolt auctioned Norica .410 shotgun. Standing well downwind of a low and straggly hedge, a large covey of red-legs was driven over him. His first shot killed a bird well out in front, and holding the gun upright he worked the bolt to reload as they flashed over his head, he dropped the second bird as the covey receded into the distance – a left-and-right at driven partridge with a bolt action .410!

Shortly after his first shoot, Tony and Marilyn moved south towards Grantham where he took the job of farm foreman on a large arable farm. This land, and our shooting adventures on it, are described in more detail in my book *'I'll be Back in an Hour!'*. It was the ground on which we shot many pigeons and in later years, I learned my fallow deer stalking through the hard school of experience, trial and error.

Before each of our children was born, we had already decided on a boy's or girl's name so that the baby had an identity when it drew the first breath. Thus Jennifer came into this world on the day after the whole of the east coast had been ravaged by a severe overnight storm, during which many buildings in Kirton suffered damage. Thankfully our house remained unscathed although next-door's greenhouse and garden shed were strewn haphazardly all over our vegetable plot. Of more importance to our immediate needs, the road to Scunthorpe hospital was clear, as Shelagh promptly went into labour, and in her condition she did not take kindly to my suggestion that we should re-name our daughter Gail as a tribute to the weather conditions that had brought about her arrival!

Two years later, Lorraine arrived on the scene, and I brought mother and baby home from hospital through a snow-covered March landscape. Now with the added responsibility of two extra little mouths to feed, I began looking for a more senior teaching post in a larger rural school, and when Lorraine was barely six months old we moved south to Wiltshire where I was to lead a larger geography/geology department in a rural comprehensive school of just over one thousand pupils.

In all we had spent four years in Kirton, and in that time I had become a dedicated rough shooter. Though now reasonably happy that I shot game birds and pigeons on the grounds that the former were often artificially stocked and the latter were an agricultural pest, Shelagh found it harder to accept the shooting of the truly wild birds which formed the wildfowler's quest, and I did not really push the idea. In the year that Lorraine was born, I had, however, applied to join my local club, the Gainsborough Wildfowlers Association, and two weeks before we moved south I received notification of associate membership on payment of the appropriate fees. It was too late, and we were now moving to a new location in central Wiltshire that was a much greater distance from any foreshore.

CHAPTER 7. ROOTING IN WILTSHIRE.

housing. . . .the DLA rough shoot. . . . .riverside duck. . .deer and deer stalking.. . .my first Canada goose. . . brother's cottage.. . . .,- return to the Dyfi. . . . .. .pressure from Arthur. . .the re-awakening. . . . .end of an era..

We faced the problem that anyone encounters when moving from 'the north' to 'the south'. House prices were so much higher in Wiltshire and the house we had vacated in Kirton took nearly eighteen months to sell. As my new school stood between two large army camps and a substantial number of pupils were from military parents, my new head-teacher persuaded the military authorities to let us move into a vacant officer's married quarter until our house in Kirton was sold and we could buy a property within commuting distance of the school. Coming from our inter-war semi in Lincolnshire, we moved into a large detached house allocated to the rank of Lieutenant-Colonel. Our furniture barely filled half the new house! Inevitably, when we moved out two years later, having filled every room with appropriate furniture, we had to shed a considerable amount of goods and chattels in order to fit into the little house we purchased at the far end of Salisbury Plain in Westbury.

Our rented house stood amid a row of three on the 'back road' which ran northward along the valley of the Wiltshire Avon. From our bedroom I could see my classroom, one of the three geography rooms that occupied the top floor of the main school block a few fields away on the far side of the river. Thankfully, we were surrounded on all sides by farmland, on the edge of a village and some distance from any military enclosure. One morning I glanced out of the window to watch a roe deer, the first I had ever seen, being chased across a field by a group of curious heifers, and in the appropriate season we were kept awake on many successive nights by the unearthly screaming of a vixen advertising her presence in the small conifer plantation at the far end of our garden.

Late one Saturday morning when I was fully occupied with domestic and family matters, I heard gunshots from behind the house, and I went to investigate. At the end of the conifer plantation were a number of parked cars towards which some Barbour-clad shotgun shooters were converging. My questions identified the group as the Defence Land Agent's syndicate, and I was directed to Harold, the secretary and chief organiser. A glance around the group quickly highlighted the difference between this syndicate and Baz Glover's motley crew. This was definitely 'English side-by-side' country and a Barbour 'Solway Zipper', tightly belted at the waist, was the 'de-rigueur ' accepted uniform. Harold eyed me suspiciously, and through coils of cigarette smoke on that still winter's day, he probed deeply into my background when I asked if there were any vacancies. Two factors counted in my favour, I was a teacher in the local senior school, and I lived virtually on one of the syndicate's patches of ground. On the other hand, I felt the mention of my name, and that another member of the group who had joined in the conversation identified me as a regular contributor to the *Shooting Times* magazine, really counted against my appeal for membership! Nevertheless, as requested I submitted a written application, and two weeks before the end of the season I was invited for a day's shooting.

It had snowed quite heavily during the day before we gathered near some riverside fishponds about five miles upstream of our home. The snow had crisped in the sharp overnight frost and stalactites of ice sparkled in the morning sunlight from overflowing guttering in the nearby village and from the branches of the trees that sheltered our car park.

While Harold briefed the assembled members and outlined his plans for the day I took in the wintry scene around us. The river, famed for its chalk-stream trout fishing, slipped silently past, oily, grey, and apparently lifeless between its reed-fringed banks. From upstream came the occasional muted crash as snow, gently melting in the brittle sunlight, slipped off the branches in the riverside woodland, and across the river a small marshy field, a water meadow with its numerous tussocks of soft rush showing through the diamond-sparkling white covering of yesterday's snowfall, was to be the first drive of the day.

Harold introduced me to the group in what I came to recognise as his usual perfunctory way, 'This is Robin, he's with us for the day'. From the sea of unfamiliar faces one approached to question me about my gun, 'I say!' he said on shaking my hand, 'you've got one of those up-and-over jobs!' referring to the Baikal. 'What make?'. I told him it was Russian and his eyes glazed over, 'Good Lord! So they're making shotguns as well!' he muttered as we were directed to our positions.

Like the syndicate in Lincolnshire, this was a rough shoot organised on a 'walk-and-stand' basis, and I was allocated a position as a standing gun for the first drive. We formed a horse-shoe around the top end of the field before the walkers came from the downstream end. 'Look out for snipe!' a neighbouring gun warned me as I took my position, though a glance across the snow covered field did not seem to hold out much promise. I had not noticed that the field was crossed by two stream carriers, narrow and deep-flowing little channels, and it was from one of these that a dozen or so mallard sprang when figures appeared dimly against the low winter sun on the far end of the meadow. Quacking loudly and clawing for height on whickering wings, they slipped out to the side of the field, avoiding the walkers and the standing guns. I was watching the duck depart when the call 'Snipe over!' brought me back to reality, too late, as three of these small wading birds swept over my head. Looking back to the field, ahead of the line of walkers the air seemed to become alive with little white twinkling flashes as the low sun caught the undersides of snipe wings as they twisted to and fro in their flight. Staccato gunshots from all round the horse-shoe and in the hectic melee I watched one or two snipe fall. My own two spent cartridges had failed to connect, but I was relived to see many other misses from the other guns. To my surprise, as the walkers approached the standing guns, many snipe were returning to the field in wisps of ten or more, pitching back onto the ground from which they had been just recently disturbed.

The rest of the day was spent in the woodlands and field margins along the chalk stream's watercourse, and both pheasant and mallard were brought to bag, together with a sprinkling of unwary pigeons and a single woodcock. For my eight cartridges I had contributed one hen pheasant and two woodpigeons, and I felt that I could fit in with this group of shooters. Although there was nothing like the numbers of game birds I had seen on Baz Glover's ground around Kirton, and the average bag for a day's shooting was considerably smaller, this syndicate worked hard for their birds and I was struck by camaraderie which made the day so enjoyable. After the final drive the bag was laid out in the snow, and an aged member of the syndicate proceeded to pull the central tail feathers out of every cock pheasant. 'What's he doing?' I whispered the question to the person standing beside me, and the answer in reverential tones explained all, 'That's Frank Sawyer, he needs the feathers for his pheasant tail nymph'. So here was the creator of a legendary trout fly and author of learned volumes on chalk stream fishing

At the end of the day Harold took me quietly aside. 'We've been watching you closely all day,' he said between puffs on his cigarette, 'I expect you've been on best behaviour as it's your first time out with us, but we're happy with the way you carry your gun. One of our chaps is leaving at the end of the season because he's moving away from the area, so would you be interested in a half-gun next season?'

Salisbury was our local shopping venue, and where the Avon flows through the city there were always hoards of mallard and a few other duck showing distinct farmyard parentage, lining the riverbanks and begging crumbs from pedestrians. With such an obvious surplus in the local duck population, this brought a reluctant approval from my wife that shooting mallard in the coming season would be acceptable. All the way through our marriage, she had come to slowly accept shooting sports, but Shelagh's final 'road to Damascus' moment came when we took the two girls to visit the local livestock market where they could watch the animals. It was her first visit to such an event and she was quite visibly shaken by what she saw. Both Jennifer and Lorraine also sensed the distress of some of the animals and came away quite unhappy. As we returned to the car my wife turned to me with an earnest look in her eyes, 'I would far rather eat anything you have shot' she said, 'than the products of what I've seen here today'. From that moment Shelagh became a steadfast supporter and defender of any country sports activities that put 'wild' food on the table.

I held my half-gun membership of the DLA syndicate for ten years, during which time we had moved from our rented house to a small home of our own in Westbury, our son Stuart had been born, my first book, 'The Sporting Shotgun' was in print and I was deeply involved with deer stalking and management in a number of local woodlands and on Tony's ground near Grantham.

Out of the blue, a letter arrived from my brother Jim. For various reasons we had not been in contact since my days in Reading and I knew he had undergone a rather unpleasant divorce. Although he was still teaching in

I became actively involved in deer stalking and management

London, he had now built his dream by completely refurbishing a stone cottage actually on the sea wall overlooking the Dyfi estuary, and was planning to retire at the earliest possible date with his partner, Christine.

Late one October evening, replete after a huge meal and much wine, we sat on the railway embankment a few hundred yards from the cottage. Night had closed around us and a cold north wind bore down from the slopes of Cadaer Idris, driving swift-moving clouds across the face of the full moon. The rising tide was alternately bathed in silvery moonlight or masked in cloud-shadow, and over the soughing of the wind which sent cats-paw ripples hissing through the reeds and spartina of the saltmarsh before us, my heart rejoiced to hear the whistle and churr of wigeon as a large pack passed overhead in the darkness.

Oystercatchers burst into high-pitched discussions on the tide's edge nearby, and a large shape swept dimly over us in a bright patch of moonlight, it banked to get a better look at us before continuing on its way with a loud rasping and questioning curlew call, 'Now at last', my wife admitted, 'I'm beginning to understand why you have talked so nostalgically about wildfowling over all the years I've known you.'

When we left Jim's cottage, I brought away the family's 16 bore,- he had taken care of both the 16 and the 20 after Penyrallt was sold. By this time I had also acquired another shotgun for my children.

Shortly after moving south I visited a local gunshop one day in order to buy a waxed cotton jacket. In the gun rack behind the counter was a hammerless double with barrels so narrow I first took it for a .410. The shop owner corrected me, 'It's a pre-war Belgian 28 bore, and no, it's not for sale'. The story that he unfolded was of a person he had never seen before dashing into the shop one day, handing him the gun, asking him to hang on to it until he had obtained a shotgun certificate. He then dashed our again without leaving any details of his name or address. Four years had elapsed since that event and nothing had been heard of the man in a hurry. I lamented the fact that the gun looked un-cared for in the rack, and offered to take it home for a good clean-up. Surprisingly, the shop owner accepted my offer, on the proviso that it would be returned immediately if the person returned to claim it, and the 28 bore came home with me. In the following eighteen months I visited the shop regularly and heard no further news. Then, on another visit the shop owner announced that the gunshop was due to close during the following week. My heart sank, expecting a demand for the return of the gun, 'What about that 28 bore?' I enquired. He smiled, 'What 28 bore?' was the reply!

Both Jennifer and Lorraine fired their first shots with the 28 by the time they were ten-year-olds, and Stuart's first pheasant and mallard also fell to this little gun.

As prospective parents, we were interviewed by the head of the Junior school that Stuart was due to attend. After the discussions about class sizes, the curriculum, and sporting facilities, he focussed on my tie. 'I'm in a syndicate near Swindon' he said, obviously recognising the BASC logo, 'we've got a real problem with Canada geese on our flight pond, and we're planning to shoot it hard in two weeks time to reduce their numbers – would you like to come along?'. 'Our only proviso is that you must use cartridges with at least 1¼ ounces of No 4 shot. After all, these are big birds and to use any less powerful ammunition would just increase the wounding rate'. I wish everyone shooting Canada geese in the UK followed the same guideline!

Canada geese were new to me, and I was astonished by their size!

On a cold and dull Saturday morning I came to realise just how large these geese are, and how their size leads to other deceptions. Five years before, I was told, a pair of Canadas nested by the flight pond for the first time. This soon increased to three pairs, and also attracted geese from all round the local area so the corn scattered in the water margins for duck was being devoured in unsustainable quantities, and the geese had now taken to raiding the nearby pheasant feeders. Quietly we spread out to form a large arc around, but some distance away from, the pond, and when all was ready, the beaters and dogs were signalled in. With much cacophony of honking and quacking the wildfowl lifted off. Small parties of mallard and pochard wove rapidly shifting patterns above the skeins of geese that lumbered into the air – a spectacle almost reminiscent of scenes from the 'Battle of Britain' film. I was well behind with my first two shots as I found it hard to comprehend how these great giants of the air could fly so deceptively quickly. Within a few minutes and four more cartridges later, it was all over and I walked back to pick the first goose I had shot since that foggy morning on the Dyfi. It was a big old gander and weighed in at 14 lbs! With three Canada geese in the boot of my car, I drove home happy with the thought I could shoot this species without any conscience about declining numbers, but not relishing the prospect of spending most of the following day on goose-plucking duties.

Lying flat in a muddy Dyfi creek, Arthur didn't take to wildfowling

I made one other visit to the Dyfi after Arthur expressed a keen interest to give wildfowling a try. Staying at Jim's cottage, we re-visited the saltmarshes of my youth and although he did not really take to the sport – there was too much mud and too few birds for his liking, for me it was like a re-awakening. Somehow, the call of wildfowl and the smell of the saltmarsh had infected my blood and although the estuary was now controlled by wildfowling clubs and was no longer the 'free-for-all' of my youth, I needed to get out onto the saltings again.

All these feelings had to be side-lined, however, because of more immediate concerns. Financial worries were top of the priority list, and a mortgage interest rate of 17% caused me to cut out all unnecessary expenses. I dropped out of the DLA syndicate, sold all my guns except the family 'heirloom' 16 bore, my children's 28 bore, and one stalking rifle, and relinquished my treasured collection of sporting books. The pressures and demands of a growing family, a change of job where I was teaching in a grammar school in Surrey, working away from home and returning only at weekends, and all manner of other factors caused many tensions and disagreements, and our marriage was on a downward spiral which lasted almost a decade. Finally, when both girls were in university and Stuart was heading into the GCSE years, after twenty-seven years of marriage, Shelagh finally packed her bags and left, leaving me with a house in negative equity, a teenage son, and much heart-searching.

I like to think that I am a 'survivor', and my mission over the next few years was to throw myself into my work - my household was now down to a 'single income' after all, to look after my son as well as I could, and to pick up the scattered pieces of a life in disarray.

I was determined to start all over again.

Part 3. . . .the Clarissa Effect

CHAPTER 8 RETURN TO WLDFOWLING

rejoining the syndicate. . . . .meeting Pam. . . . Clarissa on TV. . . .Golucester Wildfowlers. . . . ..first visit to the Wash. . .. . . .fog and moonlight. . . .the engagement ring

I had resigned from the DLA syndicate twelve years previously. Commitments to earning a daily crust and keeping a roof over my family's head, together with the pressure of family life meant that I simply could not spare the finances or time on Saturdays for shooting. For more than a decade my shooting forays had dwindled to occasional hours snatched for pigeon decoying, dawns out in the woods stalking roe while the rest of the family slumbered, or the rare invitation to walk the hedgerows for pheasant on a local farm. I had sold all the shotguns except for the 'family heirloom' 16 bore and my children's 28 bore. Although my three children were taught safe gun handling and fieldcraft as they accompanied me on my rare forays, my shooting was at a very low ebb.

Now, with a change of career which allowed me to escape from the classroom, and as a recent divorcee with the youngest of my three, by then a very untidy teenager, still with me in the family home, I was in a position to look for expanding my opportunities. I had lost contact with my old shoot, but some phone book research and a call to Dave Nobbs, the present Shoot Captain, in early September brought an encouraging response. Yes, he remembered me from years past and would have a word with the Committee to see if space could be made for an additional member. I waited for his phone call with much trepidation. Just over a week later, when I was beginning to lose heart, Richard Barry, the Shoot Secretary, phoned with instructions to pay my subscription immediately, and he would meet me on the first 'duck flight' of the season on the following Saturday!

With only two small-bore shotguns in the cabinet, for duck flighting I needed a 12 bore, and quickly! The local gunshops were unhelpful, the only weapons in my price range were secondhand autos, hardly suitable guns for what was (and still is) a predominantly 'side-by-side' syndicate, so in desperation I turned to the 'free-ads' paper. Within hours I was the owner of a Lincoln 12 bore over and under shotgun which had seen better days but could nevertheless be brought back to workmanlike condition through careful stripping and cleaning, copious oiling, and much 'elbow grease' applied to the stock.

I also needed a shooting coat with rather more 'shoot cred' than my ex-military cammo and non-waterproof stalking jacket. The local open-air market provided, at a knock down price, a waterproof and breathable tweed coat that seemed to fit the bill and me quite adequately. With less than twenty-four hours to the first shoot, I had my 'new' gun and coat, and felt ready to rejoin my syndicate.

We met in the early evening at the old barn by the river. Greeted like the proverbial 'prodigal son' by Norman and Tony, two of the older shoot members, there were many unfamiliar faces and I was eyed with some suspicion,- who was this stranger with an obviously new coat and one of those 'up and over' guns, suddenly admitted to the shoot under 'emergency rules'? Asked to say a few words by way of introducing myself after the Captain's safety briefing, I felt more at ease as we dispersed to our allocated positions along the river to wait for mallard returning from the corn stubbles.

I stood on the riverbank in the shelter of a small willow. Beside me the chalk stream gurgled quietly to itself as it negotiated a graceful meander through lush water meadows, trout and grayling were dimpling the surface at the evening rise. Several minutes after my arrival, a moorhen skittered out of the reed bed by my feet voicing its objection to my presence with much scolding and indignant tail-twitching before it disappeared into the undergrowth on the opposite bank. Dusk was settling gently on the mellowing early autumn landscape when the distant creaking quack of a drake mallard came from up-river. Out of the pastel sky two duck were heading my way.

At my shot one crumpled into a ball and dropped into the river with a hefty splash thirty or so yards above my position. I was so delighted and surprised that I didn't fire the second barrel, but now set to working out the retrieve. Gradually the duck drifted down the stream, catching the slightly faster current bringing it to the outside of the bend and closer to my bank. In my wellingtons I took one pace into the reed bed but the bird was still well out of reach. Still, the ground underfoot was reasonably firm, so I took a further step towards the water's edge. This time the water reached up beyond my boot to my knee, but despite this wetting the duck was still tantalisingly just beyond my grasp. Oh well, reasoning that my first duck in the syndicate for twelve years was worth two wet feet, I took another step. This time, water replaced the muddy ledge underfoot and I was suddenly standing navel-deep in chalk stream, holding the gun clear of the water with one hand and checking that the documents in the chest pocket of my new coat were still above water level with the other. I looked down to find the duck, a fine drake mallard, bobbing gently against the buttons of my shirt.

I cannot recall how I scrambled back onto the bank, but I now stood with gun and duck, completely and thoroughly soaked from waist down, while water cascaded out of my coat and my boots overflowed. One fact became quite clear to me immediately,- the waterproof membrane in the coat which is there to prevent water getting in will also prevent it getting out! While my cartridge and hand-warmer pockets drained steadily, the water in the body of the coat sloshed around as I tilted myself from side to side. I made my way slowly back to the barn, squelching every step of the way and still carrying what felt like several gallons of water in my coat.

My reception was, I thought, unsympathetic. For example, I was asked if I had a water abstraction licence, whether I had any poached trout or grayling secreted about my person, and whether they should put a pollution alert downstream. To cap it all, Ricky, my neighbouring Gun, pointed out that he and his dog were only fifty yards downstream and ready for the retrieve. He had witnessed the whole episode with some puzzlement. Some even claimed that I had wanted to make a big splash when I rejoined the syndicate, but amid the banter and laughter I didn't care. I had shot the first duck with my new gun, the new coat had quickly lost that pristine new-boy-on-the-shoot look, and I was back among friends. I was happy.

Fashions may have changed during my absence from the syndicate, but the camaraderie, and ethos of working hard for a small bag remained. This photo was taken on a 'red-letter' day with 25 pheasants, 4 mallard, 1 'Canada' and 10 pigeons

However, in the long and dark evenings of the approaching winter I must confess that after a long marriage and with the two older children gone I was lonely, and needed someone with whom I could share my enjoyment of the countryside and the pastimes in which I was deeply involved. Working all hours I could to make ends meet, I had scant opportunity to 'go out and meet people', so out of curiosity I contacted 'Just Woodland Friends', which, despite sounding like a society of 'bunny huggers' , was an introduction agency advertised in the sporting press and established specifically for single people interested in country sports. By return I received a large folder with the details of ladies 'matched' to my age and hobbies. Like me, most were divorcees with children, all claimed that muddy boots were their preferred attire, and all, in gentle and sensitive self-written profiles, were looking for someone to share their lives. There was one that stood out from the rest in her forthright and confident approach. A horse owner and puppy walker for Guide Dogs for the Blind, she was a confirmed 'country girl' and stated her wish to become actively involved in shooting as she had acquired a young working springer spaniel. She ended her profile with the words, 'If you want to find out more, you'll just have to ask!' This was a challenge I couldn't ignore!

Of all romantic locations, Pam and I first met on the 'safe ground' of a motorway service station. We went for a long drive in her car, touring Weston Park and the surrounding countryside, giving her gangly young springer spaniel and guide dog retriever puppy a run in the process, before dining in a rustic pub. All the while we talked earnestly. Life-history backgrounds were painted in, present life-styles described in detail, and hopes and aspirations explored. Somehow, without feeling the need to explain, excuse, or justify my enjoyment of all manner of shooting sports, I quickly felt completely at ease in her company. When we parted, with the image of her ridiculously blue eyes still fresh in my mind, I felt sure my car was travelling several feet above the asphalt of the motorway on the journey home.

Three weeks later, Pam came out for a day on the syndicate shoot. During the course of the morning she stood or walked at my side, and even though I was keen to impress her with my skills with a shotgun, I seemed incapable of hitting any flying bird! However, her little springer spaniel, Molly, made her first ever retrieve - a partridge that the other dogs had failed to find, and for the afternoon Pam and her two dogs were asked to join the 'beating line'. By the last drive of the day it had started snowing heavily, and at the call of 'All out ' Pam emerged smiling from the end of the dense and difficult beat, muddy and covered with nettle and bramble fronds and with large snowflakes beading her hair. To my eyes, no lady in any finery could have matched that image, and my heart was lost!

With regular appearances on shoot days, Pam soon became an integral part of the syndicate to the extent that at the end of the season she was made an Honorary (non-shooting) member.

There we were, quite satisfied with enjoyable days out with our rough shooting syndicate, and my forays with a rifle for rabbits or deer. Living in the depths of Wiltshire, I described to Pam the wildfowling experiences that had receded into distant memories of my youth. Dawns and evenings on the Dyfi estuary or on 'the Point' at Laughrne Ferry, had infected my blood with the growl and whistle of wigeon packs and the distant sound of geese, but these had been pushed back into the darkest corners of my mental filing cabinet. I had become content, with Pam and Molly by my side, with shooting the fat stubble-fed mallard coming to our chalk-stream water meadows with the

106

knowledge that once, long ago, I could call myself a wildfowler.

Then along came Clarissa Dixon-Wright! In one of her television programmes I saw her sloshing over saltings and slithering through mud creeks, and distant memories were stirred. Then came the sight, and dammit the sound, of wild geese! Great skeins jumping out of the television and clamouring through the skies of my mind's eye. Then this 'fowler comes on-screen and declares that geese numbers had increased dramatically over the last thirty years. This statement shook me to the core because almost that long ago I had made the decision not to shoot grey geese,- I had seen them disappear from the Carmarthen Bay estuaries and their numbers dwindle on the Dyfi. In the next few days I checked reference libraries and recent wildfowl reports, and the statistics confirmed the accuracy of this 'fowler's statement,- it seemed that there are now more pinks overwintering in this country than even in the pre-war 'golden' years. There was nothing for it, I had to get back out on the saltings,- I could even smell them again!

A phone call to BASC Southwest's John Dryden put me in touch with Gloucestershire Wildfowlers, and the BASC's website pointed me to Spalding and the Wash. I had decided on this two-pronged approach on the basis that the Severn was close enough for the occasional evening flight, and the Wash was to be the venue for weekend expeditions after 'pinks'.

I decided that my recently acquired English sidelock, bought from Pam's gunsmith friend Jack Smith, although very effective against pheasant and inland mallard, had no place on the coast, so I obtained a 'rescue gun' from the scrap bin of a local gunshop. For the princely sum of £50 I was given the stock and action, and the barrels just happened to fall into my bag! What an unshootable wreck! When assembled the action was so loose that I could wedge a playing card between the barrels and the breech face, and the woodwork bore all the signs of heavy abuse. However, the barrels were still in proof and only lightly pitted, so Jack fitted an oversize hinge pin and generally tidied up the action, while I added a recoil pad and lavished attention on the wood, the result of which I became the proud owner of a clean and sound Laurona side-by-side 3" magnum.

My appeal to Gloucestershire Wildfowlers brought a proposer and seconder, and I was delighted when an 'Associate Member' card popped through our letterbox. Our first outing was not really 'true' wildfowling,- 'Ginger' my proposer, took us onto the flooded pastures alongside the Severn, and the wigeon, teal, and pintail obligingly arrived in droves, but only after it became too dark to see them! We returned empty handed and clean-barrelled, but Pam and Molly had heard their first packs of wigeon at close quarters.

For Pam's birthday, I suggested that I whisk her away for a 'dirty weekend',- wallowing around in the mud of the Wash in mid January! Accommodation sorted, shooting permits bought, the Friday evening saw us ensconced in a pile of rubble on the edge of a deep creek and far out on the saltings. Without knowing how the tides flowed on this vast area of saltmarsh, on this new ground I took every care to ensure we had an easy and safe escape route from the marsh in the darkness In the deepening gloom Brent geese in great numbers barked from the tideway and the redshank and curlew, shouting their noisy objection to our presence, kept Molly at full alert until it was too dark to shoot. Throughout the evening the distant sound of gunshots, some sounding 'heavy', along the sea wall told us where the pinks were flighting,- none came close to us but even so, I thrilled to the sound, and briefly the sight, of a large pack of wigeon high and heading for the tide's edge. At last, during the long walk back along the sea wall to the car we stopped in the still darkness to listen to the distant music of pinks on the move.

As we had yet to scout the area in good light, the following dawn saw us at the same hide. The still air had brought freezing fog and our hopes of meeting a 'lost' party of pinks were running high. Compared to the clamour of the previous evening, dawn was quiet, broken only by the raucous laughter of shelduck and the occasional call of a wader, but on three occasions teal flashed down the creek, disappearing into the murk before I could even begin mounting my gun. As the light strengthened we eventually decided that breakfast was calling when a party of five duck appeared out of the fog, giving me chance of only one barrel before they climbed away and vanished. A long walk round to the other side of the main creek brought Molly's first wildfowling retrieve, Pam's first muddy experience of creek-crossing, and my first wigeon for over twenty-five years!

The fog persisted all day, so we returned to the same spot for the evening, this time coinciding with a high tide. While the light lasted the fog occasionally lifted and Pam practiced her wildfowl identification, scanning the birds along the approaching tide's edge. The Brents were there in force again but no quarry species came near. Hours later we walked back along the sea wall in silence, reflecting on the sights and sounds of the day when suddenly there were pinks all around us. Parties clamouring to each other on all sides and at very close quarters,- we could even hear their wingbeats!, but in the pitch darkness that only exists in wild and desolate places far from streetlights, we saw none.

The final dawn saw us as far as we could out on the saltings. The fog had given way to a stiff easterly bringing flurries of sleet off the North Sea. As the light strengthened a small party of duck flashed up a small creek to our right and at the first shot (I missed the second barrel), my first ever Gadwall fell into a shallow gully. Molly was collecting the bird when the pinks arrived,- several large skeins, probably totalling two or three hundred, drifted along the tide's edge and settled a quarter of a mile away. Close enough to be tantalising yet remote enough to be unapproachable! I looked round to Pam, sitting mud-besmeared beside me and peering into the sleet of the east coast winter's dawn. Although she had yet to try her hand at shotgun shooting, she was becoming a true wildfowler. I asked for her hand in marriage, and inexplicably, given the conditions she was being forced to endure in my company, she unhesitatingly accepted!

My first Gadwall with my 'rescue' gun, and a muddy Molly on our first visit to the Wash

So ended our 'dirty weekend' and my first sortie below high water mark for too many years. In a total of around twelve hours on the marsh I had fired four cartridges but as always, the magic of wildfowling cannot be measured in empty cartridge cases. The call of the wild and lonely marshes had been re-kindled, and the clamour of wild geese an irresistible summons. I had left home with a girlfriend and returned with a fiancée, all because of one television programme - Clarissa Dixon-Wright, you have much to answer for!

On my return to work after our wildfowling trip, I casually mentioned our engagement to the office staff, and this brought a flurry of questions about what engagement ring I had bought. I confess that the necessity of purchasing this small, but apparently essential, item had not occurred to an old romantic like me, so I discussed the matter with my fiancée that evening. Her response was blunt,- what use would she have for a ring that risked being damaged or lost while she was mucking-out stables, filling hay nets, lifting bales, or mixing up feed? No, what she wanted as a token of our betrothal was a working-bred black cocker spaniel!

I viewed this with some misgivings,- I had a golden cocker when I was very young and it was terminally car sick every time we travelled anywhere, refused to respond to any rudimentary training, and was eventually given away to a good home. Besides anything else, as a confirmed devotee of the springer spaniel, in my opinion a cocker was just too small to be of use for any birds bigger than a partridge or teal. I conveyed these thoughts to my beloved but she pointed out that the cocker of my childhood was 'show bred' and not of a working strain,- she wanted a working dog. I wasn't convinced but she took on that determined look that any sane man would hesitate to gainsay.

Thus some weeks later, answering a classified ad in *Shooting Times* magazine we travelled down to Devon to view a litter of cocker puppies. After much discussion with the breeder and detailed inspection of the pedigree, Pam selected what looked to me like a little fluffy black ball with no legs, and I parted with a bank-balance-straining cheque. The drive home resurrected some childhood memories, for after snuggling into Pam's waistcoat for some time the puppy promptly threw up on her lap! In deference to the fact that she was really an engagement ring, we decided her pedigree name would be 'Black Diamond',- we call her 'Di'.

Molly, our springer, was nonplussed by the new arrival. She tried to adopt a disdainful air but was soon swamped into submission by a puppy barely the size of her head,- within a day she was seen to dangle an old sock over the puppy's nose to entice a gentle tug-of-war! Di settled in very quickly.

Pam's engagement ring snuggles up to an exhausted Molly

Roll the calendar on twelve months and she was showing all the fearless attributes of her breed,- no cover was too dense to prevent detailed thrashing and no dummy too hidden to seek out. Still I had my reservations that despite all Di's enthusiasm for her role as a gundog, she was just too small!

Then, on Di's first outing with our rough shoot in late January, came the 'Day-of-Intolerable-Smugness!' A large cock pheasant went over the standing guns. Hit by Ricky's second barrel it set its wings to plane down into the hedge a hundred yards away on the far side of the field,- a runner for sure. Di was sent for it. The little black shape disappeared over the small hummock in the middle of the field in hot pursuit. Several minutes elapsed and I was beginning to get anxious when I saw movement just over the brow. Something upright and narrow was waving back and forward as it came towards us. What came into view was an upside-down cock bird, its tail waving in the air, and flanked by two black flapping ears as Di returned to us at full gallop. Pam took the bird which was quickly dispatched, and the other guns congratulated Di on the retrieve. Pam looked at me but said nothing,- she didn't need to, there was a huge neon-lit 'I-Told-You-So' above her head, and for the rest of the day she was the absolute personification of the word 'Smug'.

A week later saw the cocker's first water retrieve of a drake mallard, and as Pam pointed our on more than one occasion, my prejudice against cockers had been proved groundless. As a last ditch defence, I raised the question of geese,- though Molly has no problem even with Canadas, they were surely beyond a cocker's capability?

In the gloaming of a cold November evening we heard the geese fly up-river. A shot from Gordon was followed by a call for a dog,- Pam and Di went to investigate. There followed a cameo in which a lively Canada was seen running across a field, flapping its wings in an attempt to take off, with a little black dog hanging on determinedly to its tail with her four paws locked in full-braking mode. They both reached a hedge-side ditch where the goose expired, and Pam arrived as Di was pulling it, inch by inch, back onto the field.

The final straw which forced me to concede total defeat came in the following September. Pam shot her first Canada goose, and Di, grasping hold of the wing root of the dead bird, pulled it out of a shallow ditch and then carried it back across the stubble field to Pam's hide! I was amazed,- of course the other wing, the head and feet of the bird were trailing across the stubble, but the cocker had lifted the body well clear of the ground!

Pam's first Canada goose, retrieved by Di and carried back to the hide

As I write these lines Di is now seven years old and I am surprised by the differences in the way our two dogs work,- the springer is a 'demolition bulldozer' both in questing and retrieves, while the cocker is a 'thinking' dog who seems to work things out in her head beforehand,- there have been many occasions where she has arrived late on the scene and found a bird that other dogs had failed to detect. Both have their faults that would disgrace a 'posh' shoot,- they run in, give voice when they find a bird, and become instantly deaf on sight of a rabbit,- I often hear the answerphone 'The spaniel you are calling is switched off, please try again later'!   But all this is forgiven when they bring back 'impossible' retrieves or flush birds passed over by other dogs.

Inevitably our little cocker spaniel has proved that my initial reservations were unfounded and that Pam was right all along. Di has reassured me that in the gundog world at least, size isn't everything.   Not bad for an engagement ring!

CHAPTER 9. WASH DAYS

.year two, . .a 10 bore. . . .abandon rented accommodation. . . .night under the stars. . . .caravan purchase. .. . .the Bland 'Brent' and extreme temptation. . . .the figure on the flood bank, Graham. . . . .Pam starts shooting,- first Canada goose. . . .Wash visits. . . .mis-fires and missed shots. . . . what price wildfowling?

By our second visit to the Wash during the following season, much had changed.

For one thing, with geese now uppermost in my mind I had acquired a 10 bore. We made a flying visit to Southam's as their auction catalogue listed a small number of large-bore shotguns in the summer sale. The two Tolleys went well beyond my pocket but there was one ropey looking English double 10 hammer gun which seemed to be passed over by the other viewers before the sale commenced. The barrels were so rubbed down that they appeared to be 'in the white' and the stock was heavily scarred. Taking a surreptitious look at the barrel flats I was astonished to discover that it had only recently been re-proved at 1200 bar with, unusually for a 10 bore, three inch chambers. Described in the catalogue as made by Johnson, it bore no maker's name or any other inscription other than 'Fine Damascus' on the rib, and it became mine at a knock-down price. The small batch of ammunition I ordered from Alan Myers, one and seven-eighth ounce of bismuth 3's loaded into cases cut down to fit the chambers, cost almost as much as the gun. By the time these cartridges arrived my goose gun was looking resplendent after I had lavished much attention on the woodwork and a local gunsmith had re-browned the barrels. Thus armed with two guns, I was taking the Laurona 12 as a back-up, we headed again for the Lincolnshire coast as the countryside closed down for the winter.

On our previous visit we had rented a caravan in Gedney Drove End. Described in the advertisement as 'wildfowling accommodation' , even though it was quite old in design, it was nevertheless warm, comfortable, dry, and suited our needs perfectly. We were returning to the same accommodation, but to our surprise, the old van had been replaced by a mobile home in pristine condition and was, with its gold-plated taps and deep velvet upholstery , very much up-market! We stayed overnight, taking in the evening and dawn flight before we were accosted by a hysterical landlady. Although it was still advertised as wildfowling accommodation, the owner complained bitterly that our dogs had made the place 'smell of the marsh'!

Actually, we had taken great care to hose the dogs down and dry them off when we returned from the marsh, and we had covered the plush caravan carpets with vetbed and sheeting, so it wasn't the dogs, it was us! A quick visit to the charity shops in Holbeach equipped us with sleeping bags and other bedding, so alongside the full payment for the stay, I left a note for the landlady explaining that we would not be returning. Luckily, our vehicle at the time was an old Toyota Land Cruiser, so with the dogs in the back and us reclined in the front, we had plenty of room to sleep out the remaining two nights in Shep White's car park. We did, however, make the decision to become independent of such troubles in future, by planning to buy a small caravan which could serve as a mobile wildfowling lodge in winter, and game fair accommodation in summer.

Sleeping overnight in our vehicle on the very edge of the marsh, I felt this was an excellent opportunity for some moonlight flighting, but alas conditions were against this most magical of wild sport. After a glorious sunset on our first 'homeless' evening flight, the late-rising moon sailed in an inky and cloudless night sky scattered with brittle and twinkling constellations that far outmatched any products from DeBeers mines. There was no hope of catching even the slightest glimpse of any bird on the wing against such a backdrop.

Throughout the night, the moonlight streaming in through our partially steamed-up windows lit the curled up form of Pam snuggled in her sleeping bag on the reclined front passenger seat. Added to the fitful sigh of the wind beyond the sea bank and the gentle snoring of Molly and Di from the dog box in the back compartment, the occasional distant wail of a lapwing together with the frequent music of pink-footed geese somewhere out there in the darkness brought a feeling of deep-seated happiness by just being there.

We were out in our hide well before dawn, and the moonset over the sea bank was slowly overtaken by a lightening of the eastern sky to herald the new day. I fired the 10 bore for the first time, cranking back one hammer to send a departing shot at a ragged bunch teal that flashed down the creek. My shot did not connect, and the birds flared rapidly in all directions as if they could see the charge of shot approaching!

Gently at first, the mudflats lit against the sunrise were gradually flooded by the rising tide, and the slow trickle of water draining the creek beside our hide fell silent as the water was stilled. Within minutes the creek's flow was reversed. Carrying bubbles and all manner of small flotsam in its advance, the deep muddy channel was quickly and silently filling. As the sun broke the far horizon, the tide flight was well under way, and as the flood approached we were treated to the most wonderful spectacle -   thousands upon thousands of many different species of waders provided a fly-past in the young sunlight. Lapwings and golden plover left the marsh to feed inland, curlew and redshank maintained a constant two-way traffic, and dunlin swarms patrolled along the tide's edge, now looking like an angry swarm of bees, now like a cascade of twinkling lights

A dunlin 'swarm' on a rising tide

as the low sun caught their white underwings. All the while shelduck laughed from the tideway and the cronking of Brent geese maintained a constant sound background to the piping of waders nearer at hand. The sun was well clear of the horizon when we felt a transport cafe breakfast calling, and we retreated to the sea wall and the car park, our minds still filled with the spectacle and sounds of this bright winter's dawn on a flood tide. Happily, the cafe's toilet block was clean so Pam tucked in to a hearty breakfast after a complete 'freshening-up', and within hours we were back on the marsh for the evening. During the day the weather changed. The bright sparkling sunlit vault of the morning was gradually replaced by a dull and damp layer of low cloud driven by an onshore wind, and these conditions continued throughout the night. We neither saw nor heard any pinks, but experienced a huge flight of brent geese, tantalisingly flying at a low height and passing, wave after cronking wave over our hide. Only a small party of duck was seen in the deepening gloom and we returned to the car without my even once optimistically cranking back the hammers of the old gun.

The final dawn on a murky flooding tide brought a teal to a snap shot from the Laurona 12 bore. It was Di's first wildfowl retrieve and she returned to our hide, having crossed two flooded creeks in order to collect the bird, with the ease of collecting a pigeon from a stubble field. I hardly had time to reload before she was back, proudly presenting Pam with her feathered offering.

So ended our second pilgrimage to the Wash. Four hundred miles, three cartridges, and one teal to show for the effort. Yet not for the world I would have missed experiencing the magical sunrise over the flooding tide, or the gentle moonlight watching over sleeping humans and dogs while the pink-footed geese chanted their wild music to the vast and lonely night sky.

Over the following year we made a number of purchases. A small touring caravan became our 'home away from home'. Double glazed, centrally-heated, and complete with a full awning, it was not too old to look shabby, and not new enough for us to worry overmuch about the inevitable incursion of dog prints on the carpet. During the winter months, the awning would serve as hanging space for muddy clothes and boots, and a drying-off point for the dogs before they entered the inner sanctum – in the summer the awning served as our evening 'G&T' lounge at the game fairs we visited.

This summer weekend activity took on even more importance when I changed my job. After thirty year as a volunteer helper for the BASC at shows and events, I finally became a full-time member of staff, the BASC Conservation Officer on the Somerset Levels. Not only did my new job take me all over Somerset selling the 'Green Shoots' project - in 'conservation-speak' the 'Biodiversity Action Plan' for the shooting community, but I also needed to proclaim the project's achievements to the general public through mounting displays at local and regional Game and Country Fairs

During the weekend of the CLA Game Fair I came across a wildfowling gun that had been my heart's desire as a teenager. In that era, an advertisement by Thomas Bland (Gunmakers) always occupied the inside back cover of the *Shooting Times* magazine, and this frequently featured their 'Brent' three-inch chambered wildfowling gun. A 12 bore

boxlock non-ejector, it was probably the last specialist fowling piece to be produced in any quantity by any British gunmaker, but at a price just touching £100 in the early 1960s, it was way beyond my reach. Now, standing outside a trade tent in Gunmaker's Row in the dusty heat of July, I had the chance to handle a 'Bland Brent' for the first time. Some weeks later, the same gun-dealer advertised his post-Fair sale in the sporting press, the Brent remained un-sold and the price had been substantially reduced – an urgent phone call was made! I had decided to treat myself as a celebration of my new career. As I parted with the money in his shop a day or two later, he casually remarked, 'Oh I've just remembered, it has a spare set of shorter game-bored barrels!' Thus, I felt the gun I had just acquired was quite unique and I was later able, through an article in the *Shooting Times,* to trace the original owner and follow the gun's entire history from its making in 1955!

We took three guns to the Wash in November, I was now the proud owner of two English wildfowling guns, the 10 bore and my 'Brent', and as Pam had started shooting, she naturally took over the Laurona 12 magnum. Over the three days we had seen only a few pinkfeet, I had fired one forlorn shot at a small party of Greylags and Pam had fired magnum cartridges for the first time. Although she missed the wigeon she had fired at, she seemed impervious to any effects of recoil and her confidence was growing.

I classify one morning flight as one of extreme temptation! There I was, cradling a Bland 'Brent' wildfowling gun in my arms on a cold winter's dawn on the east coast while thousands of brent geese passed over my head at a height of barely thirty yards. Wave after of wave, filling the air with their far-carrying cronking and confident in their protected status. My new career would have been short lived indeed had I succumbed to temptation!

It was on this trip that we first enlisted the help of Graham Wall, one of the most experienced and knowledgeable of today's Wash wildfowlers. We had met on our first visit, a wraith-like figure walking towards us through the fog on the sea wall as we pondered how and where to cross a deep creek. In his soft Lincolnshire accent he directed us to a point where the creek bed was sandy and firm, and Molly eventually found her first wigeon. We had met on the sea wall on subsequent visits and I discovered that here was a wildfowler with a deep knowledge and experience of the

Wash. Each time he spoke I readily absorbed more information about this wild and extensive environment.

We spent one dawn in his company, and although we saw many more geese than I had ever seen in the days of my youth on the Dyfi, no geese came close enough to offer a chance of a shot. Still, the magic of the foreshore at dawn and dusk was no less enjoyable despite returning home having only fired three cartridges to produce one wigeon. Our 'winterised' caravan was an outstanding success and gave us the freedom to explore other wildfowling areas in the years to come.

Of our wedding and honeymoon more will be said in a later chapter, but in the weeks before the wedding Pam shot her first Canada goose, and we ventured to Scotland for our honeymoon. On our return to Wiltshire we stopped off to visit Jack Smith, who had been working on a single 8 bore for me. This he handed to me so that my gunsmith friend in Somerset. Paul Atkins, could complete the project. By the time I visited the Wash again, I had a choice of my 'Phoenix' single underlever hammer 8 bore built originally by Geo Lewis, my double hammer 10 bore, the Bland Brent, and Jack had also given me a 12 bore magnum by WW Greener. Goose fever, (*anseritis tremens*) had really taken hold and I was accumulating an arsenal of goose guns!

The next visit to the Wash was different for a number of reasons.

Firstly, I was travelling solo with my springer Molly, leaving Pam at home with Diamond, our very pregnant cocker spaniel. In addition, I had decided that this was to be a 'big gun' visit and both my Bland and Greener 12 bore magnums had been left at home. Finally, for the three morning flights of my visit I had again enlisted the help of Graham Wall.

I arrived at the caravan site just after 3.00pm and following a hasty setting-up, decided to give Molly a run on the sea

wall, taking my double 10 bore hammer gun 'just in case. .!'
A brisk walk along the bank to exercise the dog, then out onto the saltings to sit on the edge a muddy creek among the sea lavender and salt grasses as twilight deepened. Suddenly, while I was straining my eyes and ears for any sight and sounds of geese, the wigeon flight started. Large packs of wigeon had passed to either side of me when I heard more of their wonderful bubbling conversation straight ahead. By now it was very dark but I cocked the right barrel in optimistic readiness. The wigeon calls got nearer and there they were, a pack of fifty plus, high and just sliding to my right overhead. Throwing the gun to my shoulder I swung well ahead of the end bird and fired. Momentarily blinded by the flash, my sight recovered to watch the bird cart-wheeling out of the sky to drop with a heavy thump onto the salt pasture,- a good long-distance retrieve for Molly, my first wigeon with the 10, and a great start to the expedition!

I phoned Graham later that evening and he offered to pick me up at 4.30am to take me to his morning flight venue. He reported that there were a few thousand geese in the area, but

Graham Wall, one of the most experienced of present-day Wash 'fowlers

worryingly, he added the comment, 'I hope you're fit, we'll have a three mile walk before dawn!'.

He was right on both counts. The walk, or should I say 'long distance stumble', in pitch darkness along the uneven track on top of the sea bank was followed by a hurried tramp out onto the saltings to find a suitable creek for concealment in this vast, flat landscape. Just occasionally, above my laboured breathing I heard goose talk far out on the mudflats and it was only this that kept me going! I found myself a perch on a mud platform on the side of the creek and settled Molly by my side. The eastern sky was beginning to grow pale as I took out my Phoenix 8 bore, checked the barrel and loaded 2 ¼ oz of No 3 bismuth into the breech, laying the gun gently on its slip in readiness for what the dawn might bring.

Suddenly there were geese calling from all directions and in the strengthening light we watched several large skeins crossing the saltings at an out-of-gunshot height some distance away. More calls to seaward and a wavering line of perhaps fifty birds were coming my way. 'These are shootable, get down!' Graham advised in his quiet Lincolnshire accent. Peering through the spartina on the lip of the creek I watched the geese approach. Hardly daring to breathe I slowly lifted the Phoenix off its slip and carefully cranked the hammer back to full cock. The geese were almost overhead and their calls filled the air when I heard the word 'Now!' and I swung the gun up to meet its quarry. What happened next is embarrassing to relate. As I tracked the barrel onto and through a goose, my centre of gravity must have shifted and I began a graceful back-slide down into the bottom of the creek. I didn't fire,- all thoughts were of protecting the gun and keeping it pointing in a safe direction as I reached the end of my slide! The geese had passed and Molly was giving me a puzzled look. After several years of trying, I had messed up the best chance I had ever had of shooting a Wash pink! I cursed to myself and apologised to Graham.

More geese were in the air, several large skeins passing high to either side of us, but here was another chance. A group of around twenty birds were flying along the line of the saltings at a height of fifty yards, and they slowly turned to come our way. This time I did shoot, but I knew as I pulled the trigger that I had 'poked' at the bird and missed behind. I consoled myself in the knowledge that the Phoenix had at last been used against its natural quarry, and that although I had missed with my one barrel, Graham had missed with two!

I did fire another shot that morning but regretted doing so,- the skein of pinks were nearer sixty yards up and really beyond the effective range of bismuth No 3 shot, and I still poked at the bird and missed well behind. By the time we packed up and retraced our steps to the car we had witnessed a morning flight of around five thousand geese and the clamour of their voices still reached us from their feeding grounds inland.

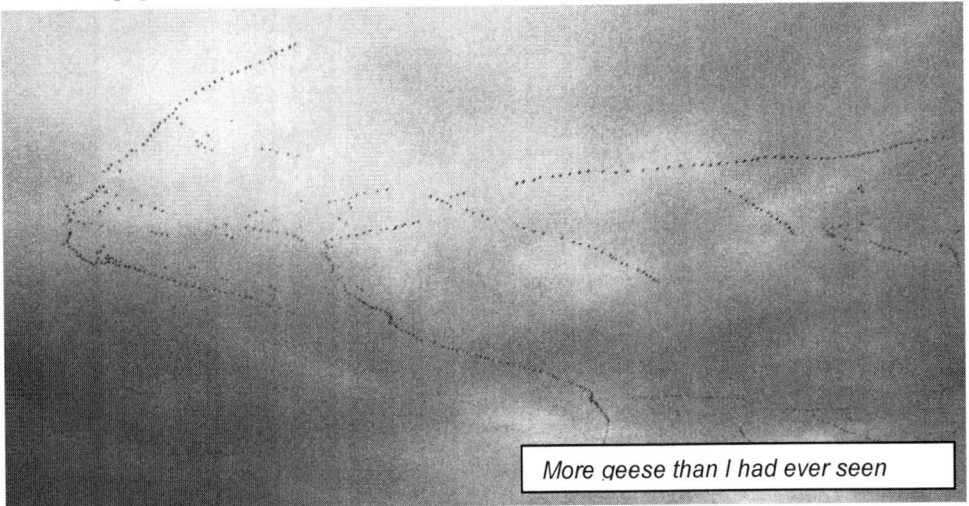

More geese than I had ever seen

The evening flight, when I armed myself with the double ten, was unproductive and I spent a sleepless night with my

127

mind filled with goose images and calls. The following morning was another 4.30 start and my hopes were running high,- this time I'll stay calm and my Phoenix will connect with a pink-footed goose!

As it turned out, a party of five pinks flew over Graham and one fell out of the sky to his single shot, but I did not have a chance of a shot throughout the flight. Still, I was happy and content to have witnessed the pageant of the dawn unfold over this wild and desolate marsh, to have had close encounters with foraging curlew and redshank, seen the 'silver rain' as thousands of knot and dunlin flew along the tideline, and watched a flight of nearly ten thousand geese! To someone who cut his wildfowling teeth on the estuaries of Wales, the sight and sounds of so many geese defied my imagination, and I'm haunted by their wild music still.

That afternoon my 'wildfowler's rest' was frequently broken with happy news from the 'maternity unit' at home,- Diamond had produced five healthy puppies and all was well with mother, babies, and midwife!

Evening flight was exciting,- great packs of wigeon roaring inland for a night of feeding on the wet pastures, some glimpsed as fleeting shadowy dots against a darkling sky. I

Wigeon and 'smug' 10 bore!

fired one shot with the 10 bore,- a large pack of perhaps a hundred birds high overhead, and a fine cock wigeon tumbled out of the clouds. I looked down at the gun and swore! Up to this visit I had not had much success with my double 10 and had decided to sell it,- but how could I possibly sell a gun now that it had pulled two wigeon out of the stratosphere in two shots? If guns could have expressions, my 10 bore was looking smug!

The final morning saw me again hoping for the Phoenix to claim a goose, and we tucked into a creek in the dark before dawn,- guns, dogs, and wildfowlers at the ready. The day dawned, and where there had been thousands of geese yesterday, there was neither the sight nor sound of a single pink-footed goose today! To my amazement, overnight they had all moved to another part of the vast marshlands that make up the Wash, and we saw not one! Wildfowlers have to be philosophical about their sport! The Phoenix will just have to wait until our next visit to 'goose country' to reclaim her birthright as a 'proper 'fowling piece'.

When I finally stepped out my car after the journey home to Wiltshire, I could swear that on the very edge of hearing I could still hear the clamour of pink-footed geese! 'Goose Fever' can really take hold on one's imagination! Now, at last, I really have a complete understanding of the term, 'a wild goose chase'.

So far in this narrative I have related the lack of success that is part and parcel of wildfowling. However, two seasons later we were again far out on the marsh having walked three miles along the sea wall in the pre-dawn darkness before striking out onto the saltings. As the light slowly strengthened a number of skeins left the Wash on either side of us when a single goose coming off the marsh to join up with a small group moving inland fell to my newly acquired double 8 bore. Molly was finally rewarded with a goose retrieve after so many hours sitting patiently and alert by my side in muddy winter saltmarsh creeks, and my first

Wash pink-footed goose lay by the gun . Graham felt a huge weight lifted from his shoulders as he had taken up the challenge of getting me to shoot my first Wash goose under his guidance, and it had taken four years! That sounds terrible, but in reality it only amounted to a total of thirteen morning flights spread over the four annual trips to the Wash, which does not seem so bad! He has already declared that his next challenge is for Pam to claim her first Wash goose!

My first hard-earned Wash pink, and the first ever to fall to an 8 bore that had spent all its life in America!

Pam and I calculated that up to now we have spent well over £4,000 on our wildfowling, yet neither of us begrudged a penny. One of our urban friends expressed surprise at our commitment and expenditure, but how can you possibly begin to explain to a non-shooter the wonder of watching a new winter's dawn unfold over the saltmarsh, the spectacle of thousands of waders in the flypast on a rising tide, or the abuse being hurled at you by a redshank as you crouch in his favourite creek. What price can you put on hearing pinks approaching in the near darkness and the adrenaline rush as you carefully crank back the hammers of your old gun,- a much greater thrill than simply slipping off a safety catch. Watching a skein of wild geese wiffle down from a dizzy height, spilling the air from their great wings as they roll and somersault, and above all, the far-carrying goose music which is the very essence of wild and lonely places.

CHAPTER 10.   GUNS

The great debate. . . . . . early days with 20 and 16. .. . first 12, the Greener GP. . . . .flirtation with repeaters. . . . .O/U on the marsh. . . . the 12 magnum. . . . .non-toxics and big guns. . .. . .effective range of bismuth/Canada autopsy. . . . ..the joy of hammers

Ask ten wildfowlers what gun they would recommend for the marsh and you will probably get ten different answers! Driven game shooters, and even rough shooters, may argue the merits of a side-by-side against an over and under shotgun or vice versa, but there are far more shotgun choices available to, and championed by, wildfowlers than any other branch of shooting sports. As a brief diversion from my wildfowling history, here I add my ha'penny-worth to the cauldron of debate. I only write from my own personal experience, and of course my prejudice and preferences are a result of these.

All right, I admit at the outset that I am a self-confessed dyed-in-the-wool traditionalist who believes that the sport of 'wildfowling' can only take place where the frosty marsh samphire crunches under your waders, the spartina is your only cover, and the sea wall is to your back. All other duck and goose shooting over freshwater and inland can be described as 'wildfowl shooting', but it is not 'wildfowling'.

. When we crest the sea wall we leave the 21st Century behind and enter a timeless world governed by wind and tide, a land of saltings, spartina grass, and deep muddy creeks. This mud is special. Unlike the mud of a freshly ploughed inland field, coastal mud is fine grained, gritty, soft, and very mobile. You will splosh though it to get to your shooting position, sit or even lie in it in your chosen concealment, and inevitably taste it in your sandwiches.

The surface of the mud is lifted by the waters of a rising tide (have you ever seen clear water in an estuary?) and deposited as a thin coating on any marsh vegetation that the tide covers. When the tide ebbs the wind dries off the plants and the mud particles are blown off in what is in effect a 'diluted' sandstorm. No matter how careful you are, your gun will get muddy as a matter of course. This happens by direct contact with the ground surface, by being handled by mud-smeared hand or glove, and even by the ingress of wind-blown particles, yet it will still be required to function perfectly when the chance of a shot comes. Therefore for those aspire to join the ranks of wildfowlers, the ideal weapon must be robust, uncomplicated, inexpensive, and totally reliable.

As you will have read in previous chapters, I first crossed the threshold into this world at the age of ten, armed with the family's side-by-side 20 bore. With its 2½" chambers it was a plain little boxlock non-ejector game gun, and the only cartridges then available from Jack 'Alma's' gunshop in Llandysul was the standard Eley '20 Gauge' loaded with No 5 shot. This load had to do for all my shooting. In order to purchase one box of 25 cartridges I had to use my entire pocket-money income over three weeks, and this taught me very quickly the effective range of the gun – any careless or long shot only resulted in the waste of a precious cartridge. I carry this legacy to this day as I am still miserly with cartridges and very reluctant to waste any ammunition on frivolous or optimistic shots! In those early days I killed a good number of duck with the 20 bore, but on the foreshore I soon came to feel quite restricted by the limited effective range of this little gun. As early as I could and as soon as Jim acquired his Greener GP 12 bore, I graduated to the 16.

With its 2¾" chambers, the 16 bore could handle the same load as a 12 bore game gun, and specifically for my wildfowling, Jack stocked 16 bore Eley Alphamax in shot size 4, and Hymax in 5's. Again the gun was a side-by-side boxlock, and in the years I used either of these guns they never mis-fired or malfunctioned in any way despite having to endure some quite appalling conditions and at times being treated rather badly!

When Jim was away in college, I sometimes took the Greener GP onto the marsh, it could after all fire a heavier load than the 16, but in the days of swollen and damp paper-cased cartridges which inevitably jammed the extractor mechanism, it soon fell out of favour!

In my teens I was much taken with what I saw as the huge potential fire-power of a five-shot repeater (legal in those days!), and for a couple of seasons a borrowed Remington 1100 was my chosen duck gun. Well engineered and with little recoil, it was a delight to use in a pigeon hide but alas, on a number of very frustrating wildfowling occasions it failed to reload for a vital second shot. Mud got in through the loading port and into the magazine, the sliding breech became very 'gritty' and failed to recycle a fresh cartridge into the chamber. Copious oiling of the moving parts made matters worse,- the mud and grit used the oil to get even further into the mechanism! The Remington was abandoned and I decided that what I needed was a five-shot repeater that I could reload through my own efforts, and the auto-loader was replaced by a Savage pump-action which I often borrowed from Raymond when he was unavailable for a wildfowling trip. Chambered for 3" cartridges, it is the gun he still uses to great effect when we make our annual trip to the Scottish foreshore, but in my teenage years I often encountered problems when I took it 'mud-larking'. Another season on and I was getting very disillusioned with all this five shot business. What was the point of all this fire-power if the gun jammed after the first, or at best second, shot? The pump action seemed good for the 'gangster and cops' movies, but was barely an improvement on the auto-loader when down on the saltings.

I had to be content with two shots so what I needed was two barrels!

My first O/U, an Italian Brevetatto trap gun

My first over and under arrived on the scene, and with it I shot a happier two seasons on the foreshore. However, there were still rare times when mud would get into the extractor and ejectors while reloading. On an over and under the barrels drop down a long way when the gun is opened, and reloading was hard enough when hiding in a cramped muddy creek. Doing so also exposed the extractor mechanism on either side of the barrels, and great care had to be taken in slipping fresh cartridges into the breech while wearing mud-encrusted woolly gloves!

Eventually my choice of 'fowling piece came full circle. I had begun my wildfowling with the family's side-by side 20 bore, and in my later teens both Jim and I acquired Zabala 3" magnum side-by-side 12 bores which performed faultlessly until I sold mine a decade later in Lincolnshire. Here was the ideal wildfowler's gun,- strongly built and reliable, it had set me back the princely sum of £35 bought new from the Grange Gun Co. Like all non-ejector side-by-sides, apart from the safety catch and top lever, there were no vital moving parts to be clogged by mud, and there were no intricate mechanisms exposed when the gun was opened,- any grit that got in between the breech and the action flats could be wiped away with a tissue or rag. There was never any doubt that it would function correctly and I always had a second shot available to me when I needed it.

Leafing through some back numbers of *Shooting Times* magazine, I came across the 'Wildfowling Number' in which a number of gun dealers were asked what they would recommend to their customers as the ideal wildfowling gun. Re-reading the article again I was dismayed to find that all but one of the dealers interviewed declared that a magnum proved semi-auto 12 bore would be their choice! My natural cynicism made me wonder if this was a ploy on their part to move stock from their sales racks, because from my own personal experience I could not conceive of weapon that was less suitable for the purpose!

A few years ago the BASC magazine ran a wildfowling gun test in which a number of autoloaders were compared. All were rated for ease of operation, simplicity of dismantling, and build quality. During the course of the tests in 'field conditions' on an estuary, every single test gun jammed, and they were even rated on their propensity to malfunction in tough conditions! Now I know there are a great many advocates of magazine-fed shotguns for wildfowling, particularly in these days of non-toxic shot regulations. In America they are the weapon of choice for waterfowling and the recent introduction of the 3½" cartridge for 12 bore has added to this popularity on both sides of the Atlantic, but somewhere along the line a vital point seems to have been missed. Unlike most forms of inland shooting, below the sea wall the opportunities for a shot are few and far between and I really do need a gun I can rely on to work properly when the rare chance presents itself. Autoloader users, according to the magazine articles mentioned above, have come to accept that jams will happen and their only concern seems to be 'how often?' – unreliability has come to be accepted as normal.

With all the other uncertainties that are integral to the sport of wildfowling, this is just one step too far for me! OK, nowadays the side-by-side shotgun has largely sunk to 'unfashionable' status, and the current shooter's taste is for flashy over and unders, or even Realtree-camouflaged auto-loaders. These high-fashion guns look very pretty on the gun dealer's rack and perform well by the flight pond or from a pigeon hide, but on the merse they could come 'unstuck' and deprive you of the only chance of a shot in the whole flight – a gun of this type sent to me for testing did exactly that on a recent visit to the Solway.

For the wildfowler in this environment, what gun could be better than a 'bog-standard' boxlock non-ejector side-by-side 12 bore chambered for 3" cartridges?

For the goose shooter, there has been a great resurgence of interest in large bore wildfowling guns - big, heavy, and noisy weapons that are capable of hurling many large lumps of 'non-toxic' into the icy dawn air from some remote sea wall. To some extent, their rise in popularity has been enhanced by the legal requirement to use non-toxic shot for wildfowling. Apart from 'heavi-shot', all other lead substitutes are lighter than lead, and therefore require a larger shot size to achieve the same down-range effectiveness. Larger shot means fewer pellets in the cartridge and consequent less dense shot patterns. To compensate for this you need a bigger cartridge with greater shot capacity, and this was the driving force for the introduction of the 3 ½ " super-magnum cartridge for 12 bores. Loaded with 'steel' shot and generating enormous breech pressures, they achieve a high velocity in an attempt to make up for the low density and 'carrying power' of steel.

I hear a lot of complaints from wildfowlers about the cost of non-toxic shot compared to the lead cartridges of the 'good old days'. Considering the number of cartridges that Pam and I use on the foreshore, the cost of ammunition forms a very small part of our overall expenditure on wildfowling. Yes, bismuth and tungsten cartridges are expensive compared to 'inland' ammunition, but it seems that we shooters have a short memory. As stated earlier, the 20 bore cartridges of my youth cost me the equivalent of three gallons of petrol. Apply that same comparison today and the financial outlay on a box of bismuth does not seem so bad! It is just that in the intervening years we shooters have become used to incredibly cheap lead-loaded cartridges at hugely discounted prices.

As to the effectiveness of these lead substitutes, I can only comment on bismuth as I cannot use steel shot in any of our guns and I have only recently started using tungsten in my 8 bore loads.

Last year I shot a Canada goose with my 8 bore. It was one of those occasions when I knew I was 'on target' the moment I pulled the trigger and was pleased that the goose folded into a shapeless heap as it fell,- it was an instantaneous kill. When dressing out the bird I found it had received two pellets in the head, one in the neck, and there were also seven body strikes. Pam boned out the bird and it was what this detailed 'autopsy' revealed that set me to some serious thinking.

Ever since the 'lead ban' came into force I have used Bismuth shot for all my wildfowl shooting. Where in the past I used No 6 lead for my inland duck, I changed to Bismuth 4's and really found no difference in my 'kills to cartridge ratio'. Perhaps with my non-toxic cartridges I was just that bit more aware of only shooting at birds I was sure were in range, and I have been even more careful to avoid the optimistic 'long shots' I was occasionally guilty of in the days of lead shot.

It must be remembered that duck in full winter plumage, whether they are inland or on the salt marsh, have a far more dense layering of feathers that the average pheasant or partridge. It therefore takes a much more determined pellet to break through the plumage, penetrate bone and muscle and cause fatal damage to the bird's vital organs. At all reasonable ranges bismuth 5's, or better still, 4's, will do this consistently and produce instantaneous and humane kills.

A Canada goose for my Phoenix 8 bore. The autopsy gave me much to think about!

Geese are an even more difficult proposition. If we take the pink-footed goose as the main grey goose in the quarry list, the 'plumage armour' is roughly the same as a well-feathered mallard, but the distance the pellet has to travel through body tissue is almost doubled, and the bones surrounding the body cavity are considerably thicker. Thus a pellet that would provide killing penetration in a mallard may well fail to reach the vital organs of a goose at the same range, coming to rest somewhere in the breast muscle or against the breast bone. The result is a 'pricked' bird which, though injured, would certainly fly on and could even survive,- X-ray images have shown that a large proportion of wild geese can carry a number of shot and still remain very active. However, the very foundation of our sport is the principle of killing our quarry cleanly and in such a way as to make it fit for eating, and the idea of a wounded bird flying on should be extremely upsetting to any sporting shooter.

So, how can we achieve a consistent killing load for geese when using bismuth cartridges? It comes down to the combination of two factors, shot size and shot load, with the added complication in that the distance from gun to bird is crucial. Basically, we need a pattern dense enough to ensure a good number of pellet strikes, together with a pellet size that retains sufficient energy to penetrate through all the barriers of feather, muscle, and bone to inflict fatal damage on the bird's vital organs.

5's and 4's, so effective on duck, simply do not have the penetrative power to be effective against any goose beyond about 30 yards. Certainly outside that range the pattern is still sufficiently dense and you may well drop a goose by breaking a wing, you may even kill one by a lucky pellet strike to the head or neck, but 'body shots' will result only in wounding.

Now we get to one of the 'standard' shot sizes for geese,- 3's. I believe that this size will extend the effective penetration range to 35 or even 40 yards, but in normal 12 bore game loads of 1 1/16 oz with only about 150 pellets per cartridge the pattern begins to get sparse. One really needs loads of at least 1 ¼ oz, and preferably 1 ½ oz (210 pellets) in a 12 bore cartridge to ensure a killing pattern. In a well bored gun throwing even patterns, N° 3's from a 1 ½ oz 12 bore cartridge will probably lose their penetration before the pattern gives out, so a goose shot at 45 yards may well be 'clattered' by a good number of individual pellets without fatal damage to its internal organs. Thus the dedicated user of 3's in bismuth really must restrict shots to birds well within range or risk an unacceptable level of wounding.

Moving up the power scale to the 3 ½ " chambered 12 bores and the 10, 8, and 4 bores,- 'proper' goose calibres, with cartridge loads upwards of 2 oz, N°1 shot really come into its own. Pattern will be sufficiently dense out to 45, or even 50 yards and for the first time this is matched by penetration. Thus I believe that this size of shot in loads of 2 oz or above should be the standard for the foreshore wildfowler in pursuit of geese.

What about BB I hear people ask? At 70 pellets to the oz the pattern in a standard 12 bore load is very unreliable even at 35 yards, and even in the big guns there is insufficient pattern density to warrant the use of BB's in anything less than a 4 bore firing 3 oz of shot. Thus I subscribe to such eminent goose shooters as Douglas MacDougall and Alasdair Mitchell in avoiding using BB loaded cartridges in any of my guns.

Going back to the autopsy of the Canada that started this train of thought, the bird was killed in a crossing shot so the distance at which it was shot and where it fell was roughly the same. I measured this carefully at 48 yards. The head and neck shots killed it, but of the seven body strikes, only two had penetrated the body cavity. . Bear in mind that this was a crossing shot so the pellets struck the bird's flank and did not have to penetrate through the breast muscle and breast bone as they would in an approaching or an overhead shot. The other five pellets were lodged deep in the chest muscle or had reached the bird's rib cage above the breast bone without penetrating further. Without the head and neck shots I am sure the bird would have flown on with wounds that were not immediately fatal. I was using an Eley 'Extreme Range' 8 bore cartridge loaded with 2 oz of N°3 Bismuth.

If you intend to go out after geese, do get a gun that will 'do the job',- a 3" chambered 12 bore should be the minimum requirement even for decoying at close range. It is a sobering thought that the 'wounding issue' has been the major factor in the banning of shotgun sports in three Australian territories, and it could well happen here. With the Canada goose 'autopsy' evidence before me, my next batch of 10 and 8 bore cartridges will be loaded with N° 1's.

Two points to take from this – big guns have the advantage of providing the wildfowler with a dense pattern of large shot, thereby increasing the chance of making clean and humane kills at normal shotgun ranges. In this age of unleaded ammunition they cannot be used to extend the range of a shore shooter as they did so effectively in the days of lead cartridges.

At the time of writing our gun cabinets hold the evidence that our goose fever has reached chronic level. We have three boxlock non-ejector 12 bore magnums, Pam's 'fowling piece is by George Lewis and I have my Brent and the Greener. Alongside the double 10 bore is my 'Phoenix'

'The joy of Hammers' The 10 bore waiting for geese on the Solway

single 8 also by George Lewis, and a new arrival, a double 8 bore by Lovell.

These last three 'big guns' have brought about a certain 'joy of hammers' to my wildfowling. All were built by Birmingham gunmakers in the late 1880s and have external hammers. There is a certain magic and thrill, as you sit in a muddy creek late into the deepening twilight of a winter's evening, when you hear a skein of geese approaching. Searching with your eyes, you also listen intently for any indication of their direction and even height. The wild music gets closer and before you catch your first sight of these enigmatic creatures, you decide that a shot may be 'on'. Carefully you crank back a hammer until you hear the quiet and well-engineered click as it reaches full cock – the geese are sounding closer still and you ponder whether it is worth cocking the second barrel. Decisions, decisions! Suddenly they are over you and you half throw the gun to your shoulder before realising that the birds, a line of indistinct shapes against the vast darkling sky, are just beyond range. The gun is lowered and carefully you ease the hammers back down to rest, and your heart rate begins to subside as the wild chorus dwindles behind your hide.

Unlike a 'hammerless' gun which is always cocked and goes 'live' when the safety catch is pushed forward, with a hammer gun the situation is almost the reverse – cocking the hammer is a positive physical act by the shooter which changes the gun from 'inert' to 'live'. In my mind it is much more enjoyable than simply pushing a safety catch forward!

I think it is quite obvious from this chapter that my choice of wildfowling gun comes down to a simple side-by-side boxlock non-ejector 12 bore chambered for 3" cartridges. It is a robust and reliable 'maid-of-all-work' which has the added advantage of being one of the least expensive to buy, particularly on the second-hand market. Our three

English-made guns cost far less than even second-hand autos, and there are many Spanish magnums by AyA, Laurona, Zabala, and others that are perfectly suitable, and which may be bought for a pittance. They will withstand the harshest conditions a saltmarsh in winter can throw at them and will cope with heavy use, and a fair degree of abuse!

For the dedicated foreshore goose shooter, afflicted with chronic *anseritis tremens* and ignoring all flighting duck for the vague possibility of getting under some geese, there is no substitute for an old damascus-barrelled big gun with external hammers. I agree with the feelings of Alasdair Mitchell expressed in his classic book *Goose Shooting*, - '. . . . . . . *you can kill a goose with a 12 bore, but it takes a big gun to slay one'*

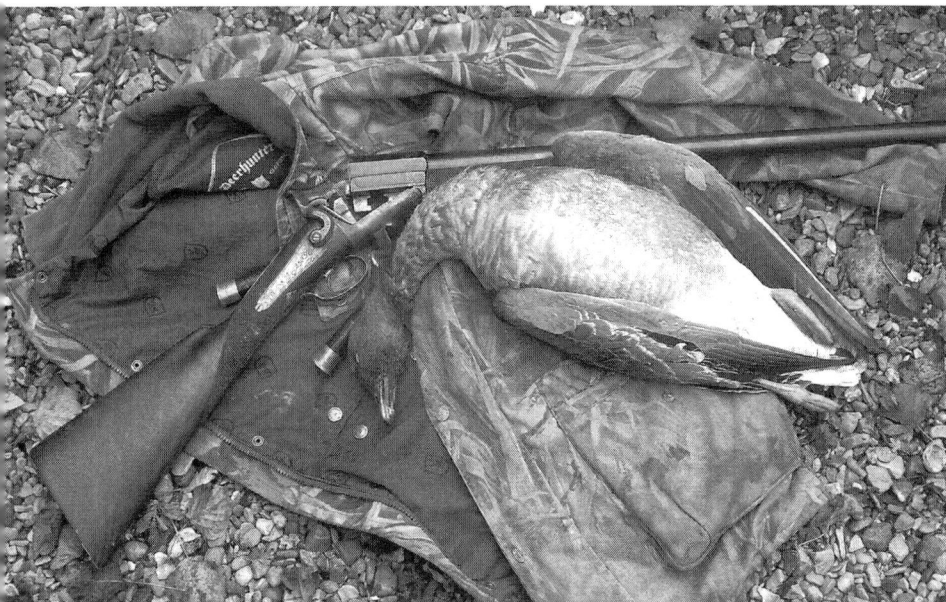

Part 3. The Clarissa Effect

CHAPTER 11. THE HONEYMOON AND BEYOND.

wedding . . . . .reluctant salmon. . . . ..Solway numbers. . . . .haunted by music. . .. .mixed barnacles and pinks. . . . .overcrowded saltings. . . .the Phoenix arises. . . . .the first goose. . . . .the Kingdom of Fife. . . . .inland decoying. . . . .the Tay and Eden,- Raymond's first pink.. . . .establishing a tradition. . . . .the Solway in September. . . .building goose numbers. . . . .the barnacles arrive. . . .January on the Solway,- a cowboy rodeo

Pam and I were married in late October. The lead up to the day was a period of frantic activity as we had decided to do our own catering, and the accent would be on food we had caught, shot, or gathered ourselves. The menu we devised sought to 'out-pretentious' any high class restaurant and included sides of double-figure trout smoked in my own cold smoker, roasted haunches of venison, an assortment of game curries, crayfish and mussels, and virtually anything else we could find in our freezer. Two barrels of real ale were donated by Dave Kenyon and a raid on Carrefour in Calais a week before provided huge quantities of wine. We catered for 140 guests and there was certainly enough to go round. On the day, while we were otherwise occupied in matters matrimonial, all catering tasks were taken over by Pam's friends Gill and Penny. After the church ceremony, the reception was hectic, with my two ceilidh bands providing the music and my old Morris team, the White Horse Morris Men, turning out in force even though I had not danced for a decade!

Late on the next day we bade our farewells to family and friends and, driving overnight, headed for Scotland. Our honeymoon luggage contained three wildfowling guns and all the associated clothing and equipment, two salmon fly rods and relevant waders, waistcoats, landing nets and bags of tackle, and two dogs. For a honeymoon, where else would we head for but the Solway Firth and the River Nith? Staying for a week in a cottage owned by Pam's gunsmith friend, Jack Smith, in the Nith valley some miles north of Dumfries, we planned to divide our time between fly fishing for 'back-end' salmon on various club waters during the day, and exploring the Solway for geese at dawn and dusk. It didn't really work out that way and we soon discovered that we had to devote each day to either fishing or shooting – we simply did not have the time to mix the two pursuits in the course of a single day.

The salmon were un-cooperative. Fishing on the mid-Nithsdale Club waters on our first day, there were fish showing all over our pool, one even leaped clear of the water beneath Pam's rod tip, but despite trying all manner of flies on various densities of fly line, neither of us had so much as a speculative pull from an inquisitive fish. I was fishing near the tail of a pool, waist-deep in water and concentrating on my line, when suddenly the hairs on the back of my neck stood on end! For a moment I wondered what was going on, and then dimly above the sibilant murmur of the river and the bubbling as the current swirled around my waders, I could hear geese. Attention on my line was lost as I looked up to see a skein of around two hundred birds, high and heading south towards the Solway. These were the first pinks I had seen in Scotland and I looked forward to the morrow, when we were to explore the foreshore.

After breakfast we met the secretary of the local club and were issued with permits while he pointed out the access points on our large-scale map. We decided to conduct a reconnaissance so that we could get the lay of the marsh before the evening flight. It was a bright and sunny day and as we walked the foreshore we took in the scenery. To me, the Dyfi estuary had always felt protected by the mountains and hills that enclosed it, the wide and far horizons and huge skies of the Wash instilled a feeling of limitless freedom, but here on the Solway it was somewhere between the two. To the south across the sands and mudflats, the land climbed hill after rolling hill to the mountains of Cumbria, behind us to the north, beyond the wind-blasted gorse and thorn bushes that edged the foreshore, the distant horizon tumbled upon itself in soft and low rounded hills. From the shoreline came the calls of waders, and a curlew wafted past us on a westerly wind. Here was a sound that was new to us, but it struck a chord from my frequent visits to Slimbridge in my previous life. Flying low across the sand was a loose gaggle of large birds, and through binoculars I confirmed that the yapping calls had come from these, the first barnacle geese I had seen in the wild.

We had just returned to our vehicle and were in the process of changing out of our boots when I heard the calls of pinkfeet. I looked up and my jaw dropped open at what my eyes took in.

Based on my experience of wildfowling on the Welsh estuaries, I had always wondered if the paintings of such artists as Peter Scott and Julian Novorol depicting huge wavering skeins of geese, line upon diminishing line fading into the distance, had an element of fantasy. I had never seen the sort of numbers painted into these works of art, and even on our recently established forays to the Wash we had not yet seen great numbers in the air. Yet here was a sight that stunned my senses and confirmed that such paintings could indeed be a reality. By the time I reached frantically for the camera the first three skeins had already passed overhead and those following, line upon wavering and ever-changing line, stretched back to the northern horizon. As well as the sight, the whole sky was filled with sound, thousands of goose voices, each one different, called, answered, instructed or guided the huge squadrons as they passed high over two enthralled humans standing on the threshold of the sea. Far out over the sands the formations broke, and as if by a signal the great birds wheeled, twisted, and wiffled to lose height above their daytime roost, providing for us mute onlookers a spectacular display of individual aerobatics.

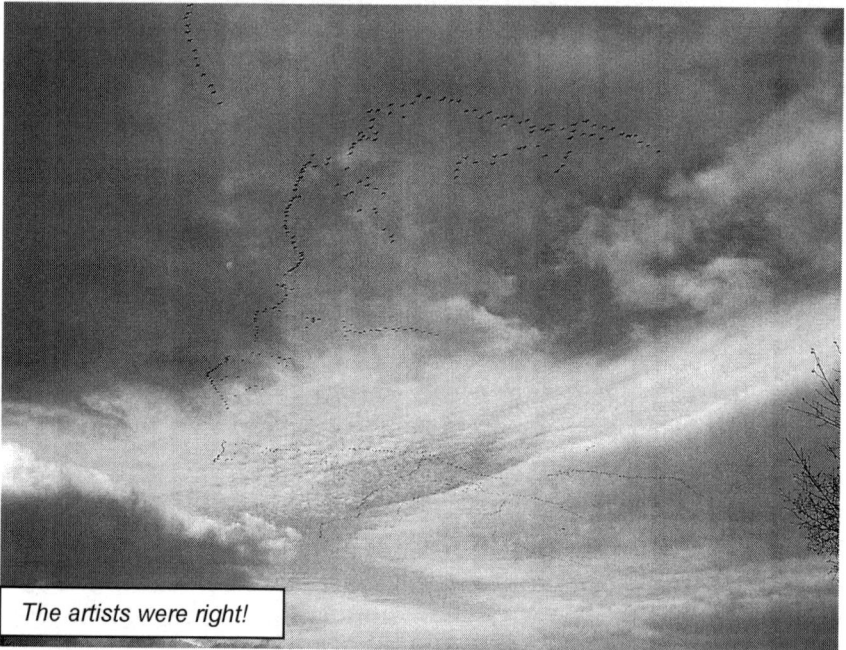

The artists were right!

We were back on the saltings that evening, and though we did see many geese, none came within gunshot. Pam was armed with her Laurona 12 bore magnum, and I had taken the 10 bore. Pam dropped into a small gully she had selected to be her hide, and I walked further along the merse to conceal myself behind a large tree trunk stranded by a storm tide. Now this may sound very silly, but as I settled into my hide and rested the old hammer gun on its sleeve across the decaying and salt-encrusted trunk, I had an overwhelming feeling that the gun had 'come home'. I have no idea of the history or provenance of my 10 bore, but somehow it just 'felt right' – the gun was back where it

150

belonged. On subsequent visits to the foreshore during our honeymoon I just could not bear to leave this gun behind, and the Bland 'Brent' did not leave its case all week.

A dull and windy dawn, and we were behind schedule. Two other cars were already parked as we drew in to the access point, and hastily we trudged out onto the saltmarsh as the eastern sky was beginning to turn pale. Pam settled into her hole, but my hide of the previous evening was already occupied by another 'fowler. Quickly I scouted round and found a suitable place for concealment further on, but I felt that it may be a little too close to the 'fowler in residence. I asked if he had any objection to my new position and he answered that he did, explaining that the geese tended to cross the saltings at an angle and I would be cutting off birds coming to him. Perfectly reasonable I thought, after all he was there first, so I went further on till I found a deep gully into which I settled.

The morning brightened, pink-footed geese crossed the coast at an unreasonable height and not a shot was fired. Suddenly a loose gaggle approached, and I could hear both the yapping of barnacles and the 'wink-wink' of pinks – a mixed flock! They swung over the saltings and in the strengthening light I picked out what I was sure was a pink-foot. With both hammers cranked back I swung onto the bird as it passed overhead, but I held my fire – I just could not be one hundred percent certain, and I lowered the gun. As I did so it opened its beak and called, 'wink-wink', probably the goose equivalent of 'Ha! That had you fooled!'

At the end of the flight my neighbouring 'fowler walked over to me. 'I want to thank you' he said, 'for moving further away this morning – it was both a courteous and sporting response to my objection earlier on'. I was nonplussed and surprised, 'Isn't that what any 'fowler would do' I asked, 'after all, you were here first?' He gave me a questioning look, 'You've not been here before have you? Just wait till you see the trippers arrive from England, when it's like

Paddington Station at bloody rush hour, you won't see much sportsmanship then!'

We ended our honeymoon trip having failed to catch a salmon, and not having fired a shot at a goose, yet with the determination to return to Scotland for more.

As far as the fishing was concerned , the various local anglers we spoke to complained that the river was too high/too low/ the wrong colour/ there were too many leaves in the water/ the fish were intent on running through/ and inevitably, we heard the dreaded salmon angler's phrase, 'You should have been here last week!'. We could take our pick of reasons for our failure, but in our defence, we did not see anyone else catch a salmon either!

On three occasions after the 'mixed flock' episode I had cranked back the hammers of the 10 bore, but each time the birds were just beyond reach and I refrained from pulling the trigger. Pam had the same experience, raising her gun to a skein only to decide they were too high to justify a shot. Nevertheless we counted our first venture north of the border as an outstanding success.

On travelling back south to Wiltshire we broke our journey to return the cottage keys to Jack. To my delight, I was handed a nearly-completed 8 bore to bring home!

I was first shown this gun some years ago. Shortly after we first met, Pam had introduced me to Jack, a gunsmith and her close friend in North Cheshire. He eyed me suspiciously at the start, after all I was a man from the 'deep south' of Wiltshire, and an ex-patriate Welshman to boot, but when talk came round to guns and gunsmithing the ice began to thaw as we found much common ground in our mutual love of English guns. It took a number of meetings, during which I often expressed my dream of one day owning an English 8 bore for my wildfowling, before he finally succumbed and produced an oily-rag-wrapped package that had slumbered in his store for many years.

Inside were the fore-end, stock and action of a single barreled 8 bore built by G E Lewis in the late 1880's.

There was a story behind these historic artifacts. Many years ago the gun had been stolen from its owner, and in time the police had recovered the pieces I was now cradling in my hands,- the barrel was never found. The owner had passed these to Jack in order that he should produce a new barrel, though with the instruction that 'there should be no hurry to get the job done'. However, only a short while later the owner died, the order was cancelled, and his widow did not wish to have the pieces back. Thus the stock, action and fore-end of this echo of the golden age of wildfowling had languished in Jack's store for many decades.

Perhaps I am an incurable romantic, but every time I handle an old large-bore wildfowling gun I cannot help wondering who had wielded it when it was newly made, what remote saltings it had visited, and how many geese had fallen to its mighty voice. In such a mood I inspected the gun parts in my hands. It was clear that it had been well cared for and protected, much of the original colour hardening remained on the action and underlever, and the stock bore few marks of abuse. From these parts a new gun could be born,- a 'Phoenix gun'.

I confess to putting a lot of pressure on Jack to rebuild the gun. After all, I pleaded, these guns were meant to be used, and it was almost cruel to deprive this one of the smell of the saltings and the clamour of geese! Possibly my words had an effect, or maybe Jack had a 'slack period' in his gun repair business, but a year later I was shown a yard-long steel tube that was to be the new barrel. By the following year it had been bored out and polished to the correct measurements, the chamber had been reamed and the lumps and fore-end loop added,- all this done 'from scratch' by the traditional method of 'sooting and filing'. By now I was getting very excited at the prospect of purchasing the finished gun, but alas more immediate demands on Jack's gunsmithing skills put 'my' 8 bore on the back burner.

As the 8 bore project had not made any further progress when we returned from Scotland, he offered to let me take the gun on so that another gunsmith could bring it to completion. Thus the re-build that started in Cheshire moved south to Somerset where Paul Atkins, a fellow member of Bridgwater Bay Wildfowlers, agreed to finish the gun.

When the jointing work on the barrel and action was complete, the gun was submitted to proof. This happened in late August, though Paul seemed reluctant to give me more details, but just as the Bank holiday approached he let on that the gun had been sent to the Birmingham Proof House. For days I paced the floor like an expectant father, when finally Paul phoned. The gun had returned from proof, and in a sombre voice he told me that the result was not what he had expected. I steeled myself for the worst, picturing in my mind a shattered barrel or cracked action. He explained that he had wanted it to be proved for 850 bar pressure, but they had tested the gun at 1200 bar instead,- by now I was convinced that things had gone horribly wrong. Then with a dead-pan voice he announced that it had passed proof! I was euphoric! With this huge hurdle successfully crossed I could now believe that my ownership of an English 8 bore had finally changed from a long-held pipe-dream to reality. Almost a year after I had brought the gun south, the first Canada goose fell when the Phoenix spoke for the first time in fifty years.

In our conversations with Raymond and my 'best man' John Dryden, our wildfowling adventures on the Solway were frequently discussed. Raymond had never been wildfowling north of the border and he was very impressed with the photos we brought back. John had not visited the Solway for two decades, and both indicated that they would like to make the trip. This gave us an idea, and when I proposed that we make up a shooting party for a Scottish trip, it was readily accepted by all.

Apart from the Canada geese in our local area, I had not experienced goose shooting over decoys, so I contacted a well-known Scottish wildfowler who put us in touch with a reputable goose guide operating around Loch Leven. Plans were finalised and a cottage in Fife booked for five people,- John and Tricia Dryden, Pam and I, and Raymond – due to her many commitments his wife Diane was unable to spare the time for the trip.

Two mornings were booked with the guide, and permits obtained for two local estuaries where we planned to spend the dusks and dawns for the remainder of the week.

We met our guide in the pre-dawn dark of the first morning. Assigned to be in a party of eight Guns, after being given a detailed briefing of do's and don'ts, we set off in convoy under the leadership of the guide's assistant. I'm not really sure of what I expected, but I did find the episode a little disconcerting. With the decoys laid out before us, the eight Guns hid behind a low embankment with only a few feet separating each, it brought to mind images of infantry in their trenches before going 'over the top'. Pam was appalled and did not even un-sleeve her gun, and for the most part I contented myself with taking photographs. A skein of geese approached, and at the assistant guide's call, 'Up and at 'em boys!' a barrage was unleashed and two geese fell. Time went on and other skeins turned away before coming within gunshot. By the time our guide called a halt to proceedings, a few minutes past 8 o'clock, my gun had been unloaded for some time.

The next morning was better. This time our party had been split into two teams of four with about 40 yards separating the teams as we crouched behind a stone wall. This, we were told, was to be a greylag morning, and so it proved to be. Hiding between a large camouflage net and the wall, John, Raymond, Pam and I waited for the coming dawn. As the least experienced shooter in our group, Pam was fearful of damaging her gun on the rough stone barrier, and again kept her gun sleeved. On three occasions greylags came in, approaching from the direction of the other team

It was a 'greylag morning'. Raymond, me, and John at the end of the flight

and after they had fired their salvo, the geese lifted past us. Both John and Raymond had birds down, and I managed a pleasing left and right, after which and much to the consternation of our guide, I put my gun away. I was happy with my two geese.

The total bag at the 'breakfast calling' halt to proceedings was fourteen geese to the party of eight Guns. We had not exceeded the bag limit recommended by BASC and insisted upon by our guide, and apart from Pam, we all had geese to take home.

Shooting geese over decoys has seen a marked growth in recent decades. On the positive side it is a way any novice wildfowl shooter can reliably expect the have a chance of shooting a goose and it has opened goose shooting to a far wider clientele within the shooting community. When carried out responsibly it serves as an introduction to geese and also serves to reduce crop damage increasingly caused by large goose populations. Unfortunately it has been tainted by unregistered and greedy guides encouraging unfeeling gunners to slaughter large numbers of geese and to harry the birds throughout the day. Enough said, I wanted to experience goose decoying before forming my own opinion, and though it was an interesting experience, it was not really my 'cup of tea'. Inland goose decoying is as far removed from foreshore wildfowling as decoying pigeons over corn stubble.

The two estuaries were different. The grandeur of a sunrise over the Tay brought sight of a few thousand geese flighting inland while the street lights

Tayside. Pam crosses the fence onto the saltings

of Dundee winked out on the horizon. Here, on one morning Raymond was traumatised. As we drew into the roadside car park some hours before dawn, there was another car already parked there so we naturally assumed that another 'fowler or two had got there before us. Silently we made our way along the field side and through the wire fence that took us onto the footpath that runs on a terrace above the saltings, which on the north shore of the Tay estuary took the form of a wide reed bed. Raymond dropped off first, then it was John's turn to seek a hiding place where the reed bed bordered the higher ground. Pam and I went further along the track so that I became the 'end Gun'. I un-sleeved the Phoenix and having checked the barrel, loaded it up and laid the gun across a fallen tree trunk just as the eastern sky took on a dim pink glow. Out on the estuary I could hear some sleepy conversation from pink-footed geese, and a piercing call I had not heard before and which I later attributed to a goldeneye drake, a duck species I had not yet met in the wild.

The light strengthened into a red dawn and from somewhere upstream I could hear someone shouting, sounding very much as if he had lost his dog and was calling it urgently! Some time later came some gunshots from the same area and I searched upstream to see what this 'fowler could be shooting at – there were no geese or ducks in the air but a carrion crow was taking some violent evasive action! Minutes passed and Pam hurried down to my hide, 'There's someone or something crashing around in the reed bed in front of me!' she said. I listened carefully and the sound was getting nearer. Was it the other 'fowler, or a deer, the 'lost' dog, or perhaps even a badger, that was making the noise? Whatever it was, it was not attempting silent progress. By now the pinks had left the estuary some miles downstream of our position, and we decided to leave the strange crashing noises as a mystery, and walk back to the car. We picked up John on the way, expecting to find

Raymond waiting for us at the car park, but he wasn't there. I went back to look for him, only to find our missing Gun walking towards me in fits of laughter. Apparently, before dawn he had decided to move out through the reed bed to the edge of the saltings, and when he attempted to re-trace his steps had become hopelessly lost and disorientated. The twelve foot high dense reed growth shut out the direction of the sunrise and obscured any view of higher ground. As a consequence he had gone round in a number of circles, crashing through the dense vegetation and wandering down to where Pam and I were concealed. He had called 'Rob!' a number of times, but from our distance the call was indistinct and we assumed his dog was called Bob! He had even fired the shots, but of course we assumed it was the 'fowler from the other car.

Tears of laughter were streaming down our faces as we drove back to accommodation, but a lesson was learned. In

Reedbed rescue – Raymond returns from his wanderings

future we all carried two-way radios!

The Eden, where the calls of approaching skeins were often drowned out by the earth-shaking roar of a jet fighter taking off from the airfield on the north shore, its afterburners cutting great blow-torch slices through the gathering dusk as it smothered goose-talk over our heads. Raymond's first ever pink came on such an evening flight, falling to his faithful old Savage pump-action, the same one I had clogged up with mud in my teenage years on the Dyfi, and Molly had her first water retrieve of a grey goose.

By the end of the week we all decided that the 'Scottish goose trip' was to be an annual event, and though we discussed the possibility combining a 'goose and salmon' foray in the autumn, it was agreed that from now on it would be a foreshore-only venture in January.

Thus for Pam and I, our wildfowling has established a pattern of the Wash in November and Scotland in January – more than this our bank account could not stand!

Last year, however, we did sneak away for a two week holiday in September. Travelling up-country at the end of the Midland Game Fair and with our caravan in tow, we spent a few days in Pam's childhood stamping ground of Whitby. At last she could get her revenge on my interminable 'trips-down-memory-lane' every time we went back to the Teifi, and her youth was re-told at every turn and corner of this famous part of Yorkshire. Botham's sausages were all she remembered them to be, and freshly smoked kippers from the ancient little smokehouse hidden away under the brooding ruins of the abbey reminded me what kippers should taste like! Needless to say, we left Whitby with a good stock of both commodities, and headed north-west to the Solway.

The last week in September marks the start of the goose build-up, or so it seemed to us. We took a walk on the saltings late on the Sunday afternoon of our arrival, and in total we saw around two hundred pinks in the evening flight. By the end of the week their numbers had built to around two thousand pinks, and late in the week the first barnacle geese made landfall on the Caerlaverock reserve, one vast pack of over a thousand birds.

Pam had settled into her hide in the pre-dawn dark, and I looked for suitable concealment about one hundred yards away, selecting a deep hollow on the very edge of the saltings. I could hear pinks calling out on the mudflats, but they did not seem to be as far out as usual. I was struggling with the straps of my rucksack when there was a roar of wings and the geese were airborne, and by the sound, they were heading my way! Frantic un-zipping of the gun sleeve and I loaded two cartridges into the magazine of an autoloader I had been sent to field test. As the geese approached I quickly worked the bolt to feed a cartridge into the chamber, and the bolt jammed. A pack of around fifty pink-footed geese sailed over my hide, obviously new arrivals and not yet 'marsh wise,' for they were only about thirty yards above me as I tried frantically and in vain to move the bolt and load the gun. The only really perfect chance of a goose in the whole week, and fortunately Pam was out of earshot as I confess to uttering a range of profanities, mostly directed at the gun!

On our return we met some friends who occasionally travel to Scotland for inland goose shooting. Their first question was 'Did you have a good time?', and as the answer was very much in the affirmative, this was followed by 'how many did you bring back?' They seemed to be a little confused by our 'nil return', in their minds the two didn't add up. I suppose there is an 'oil and water' situation here. When they proudly told us of a morning some years ago when their party of eight Guns shot more than fifty geese over decoys, they in turn were disappointed that we were not impressed!

For those who wish to do so, and here I really urge adherence to the BASC Code of Practice, shooting geese over decoys will put a goose or two in your bag, and nowadays many more geese are shot inland than on the coast.

This is a form of wildfowl shooting, but it will never make you a wildfowler. It will not teach you to respect the tide, or to read the wind, to tell the difference between a redshank and a greenshank merely by its call, to ignore the duck coming upon you suddenly in the faint glimmer of a winter's dawn, because you know it is a shelduck, and to appreciate every hard-won feathered bundle that falls to your gun.

In England and Wales, the changes in the way Crown Foreshore is managed and administered has meant that where wildfowling takes place, it is controlled and regulated by local wildfowling clubs. Through mentoring members and keeping watch over the marshes, the 'marsh cowboy' behaviour I first witnessed as a ten year old on the 'Point' has largely disappeared from foreshores south of the border. Anyone shooting indiscriminately, shooting at wildfowl that are well out of range, or otherwise making a nuisance of themselves are quickly weeded out by the clubs.

In Scotland the laws governing access to the foreshore are different, and last January our annual shooting party witnessed a cowboy rodeo at a well known Solway wildfowling venue. On one evening flight, many skeins of pinks crossed back onto the sands from their feeding grounds inland. Flying at heights of two hundred yards or more, yet they were still greeted with a barrage of shots as they crossed the coast. We watched through binoculars from a quiet spot further down the coast, and wondered if these 'trippers' only came to Scotland because they had been ejected from clubs south of the border.

By that time in the season all the geese had acquired the wisdom to gain altitude well before crossing the coast, even in high winds and driving snow showers, but we did get one or two chances at small family parties and stragglers, and the trip was again a success.

Although Tricia Dryden has far more sense than to suffer the discomfort of coastal wildfowling, she nevertheless provides valuable back-up, and is the lone voice of sanity in our shooting party. We enjoy each others' company, we have the same views on all manner of shooting sports, and the Scottish trip is now an annual fixture.

With our November trips to the Wash where we enjoy the company of Graham Wall and his wife Kathy, and the January 'Shooting Party' to the Scottish foreshore, the pattern is set for the future.

Added to the duck flighting evenings on my Wiltshire rough shoot and the evening flights on the Somerset Levels as I return home from work, perhaps two weeks' true wildfowling each season will be enough, for the moment, to satisfy my wildfowling soul. Retirement will bring a different perspective, and we look forward to moving somewhere so that, on a deep winter's evening, I can stand on the threshold of my back door and listen to geese in the night sky

In all my accounts of wildfowling adventures in this book, I wonder if I have dwelt on the lack of success rather too much. We have brought back geese and duck from the Wash and from Scotland, not every time it has to be admitted, but often enough to make us start planning 'the next time' even before we return home. Perhaps this the essence of wildfowling – nothing is certain and in this uncertainty lies much of its charm.

CHAPTER 12.   I'LL BE GLAD WHEN I'VE HAD ENOUGH!

*the big question. . . . .the American book. . . . .Pam's relief. . .
.why do we do it? . . . . . .wilderness and wildlife. . . . .solitary. . . .
.the only wild sport . . . . .extremes of highs and lows. . . .
.the call of geese. . . . .I'll be glad when I've had enough!*

How often, when you have been out on the foreshore in the teeth of a freezing January gale at dawn, sitting for hours waiting for the slow lightening of the sky while water trickles into your boots and, having slipped off your plastic sheeting, your backside is decidedly cold and wet, do you ask yourself the question, 'What am I doing here?   Most wildfowlers are in some form of denial about this, but to someone looking at the sport from the outside it really is a silly game, yet we keep on doing it! What is the ingredient which drives us over the sea wall to suffer all manner of hardships and discomfort for the sake of an occasional duck, or that greatest of prizes, a goose? To be a wildfowler one has to be a chronic optimist, and I am sure that this is a limiting factor – like salmon fishing, the sport appeals only to the limited number of people with this personality defect!

On one of our Wash trips, the pre-dawn dark of one morning saw us clambering into concealment in some stone cairns to await the coming of 'shootable light'.   As the eastern horizon began to take on a barely perceptible 'lighter shade of darkness', two other figures were seen approaching down the stone road.   A quick flash of the torch let them know our position, and they came to a halt some distance from us, though curiously, their indistinct shapes remained outlined against the dim skyline.

The light strengthened as dawn approached, but apart from a small party of teal that caught us completely off guard, no other duck were seen, though we did hear gunfire from further up the coast and the call of pink-footed geese on the very edge of hearing. I studied our fellow 'fowlers through binoculars, an older man dressed in a bright mustard-coloured waxed cotton coat held his gun at the ready while sitting on a shooting stick, and his companion stood at his shoulder with a pair of cartridges held in readiness for rapid reloading. We concluded that they were probably driven game shooters who had read something about wildfowling and decided to give it a try.

Their patience lasted not much more than thirty minutes before they left their 'peg' and sauntered over to us, 'I say,' one enquired in a rather plummy accent, 'is there anything about?' On being told that I had only seen one small trip of teal and many shelduck, they seemed a little disappointed and asked what shelduck looked like. On being given a description of the birds and told that the species was legally protected, their response was 'What a damned shame!'. I felt it would have almost been worth their while to break the law in this respect, I conjured up images of their gastronomic appreciation of this foreshore delight – having once in my youth picked up a shelduck shot by a 'cowboy' and tasted the unspeakable horror of its roasted meat! Eventually they turned for the sea wall, wishing us luck as they trudged off,- I had the distinct impression that this would be their one and only sortie beyond the sea wall and onto the foreshore! There are times, however, when I have returned from the marsh having not seen or heard any wildfowl, that I think they had escaped lightly and were the sensible ones – they had given it a try and found that wildfowling was not for them, they were 'uninfected'.

I have never mentioned my doubts about the sanity of this form of shooting to Pam, and she has taken part in all our outings without question or complaint. The turning point was reached one day, when we both 'came out' and finally admitted to each other that, while we are both infected with the wildfowling virus, the 'What-am-I-doing-here' question does occasionally arise.

What brought this on was a book. Trawling through the internet one evening, I came across an American book published by their duck-hunting and conservation organisation, Ducks Unlimited. I announced the title to Pam,' *Misery Loves Company'* subtitled, '*Waterfowling, and the relentless pursuit of self-abuse!'.* The response from my wife was shrieks of laughter and relief, 'Thank God!' she said, 'somebody else has the same feelings as I have, only until now I have never liked to mention it!'
Nevertheless, just a few minutes before typing these lines we both sat in our kitchen planning our annual trip to the Wash next week. The moon will be just past the full, Graham Wall phoned to report that the geese are in, the weather forecast predicts rough conditions, and excitement and anticipation are mounting!

On a number of occasions, both on the Wash and in Scotland, Pam has decided not to rise at 'silly o'clock' in the morning for a dawn flight, content to snuggle warm in the bed until I return. As silently as I can, I get up in the darkness and prepare to leave, only to be surprised by my wife demanding a coffee and rising from her slumbers. 'I keep on imagining' she complains, 'that today will be the day, this time skeins of geese will come over us at a reasonable height and I'll be in with a chance. Everyone will come back with at least one goose, and I'll have missed it - I can't stay in bed!' She hasn't missed a dawn flight yet!

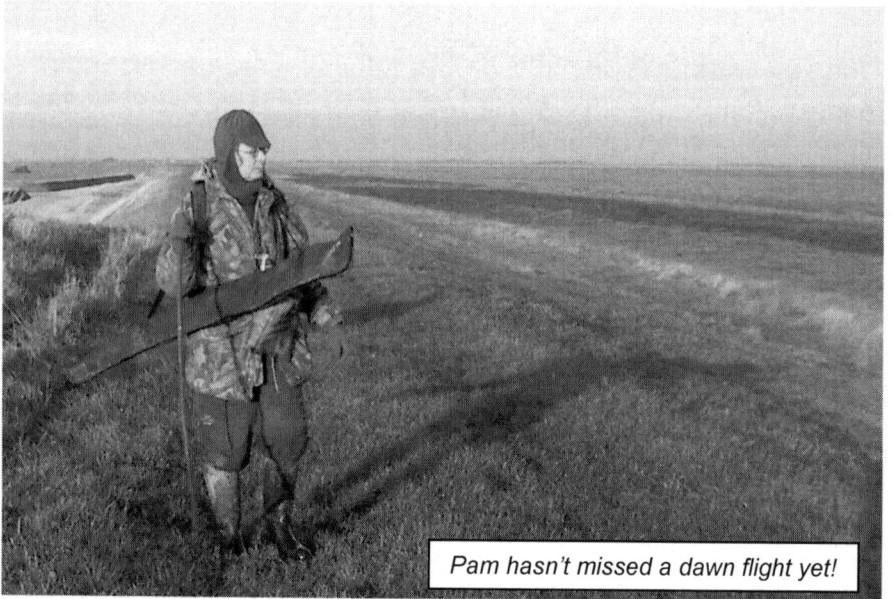

Pam hasn't missed a dawn flight yet!

So why do we do it?

Wildfowling beyond the sea wall is the last truly wild sport available in Britain. By comparison, the high heather moorland is carefully managed for grouse, and in much of lowland Britain the landscape had evolved through sporting interest in partridge or pheasant. As far as game birds are concerned, the landscape shows marked human intervention for their benefit. Beyond the sea wall, humans have considerably less influence or impact on the environment. When set against the relentless and timeless conflict between land and sea, our puny attempts to tame the landscape and control the waters can be easily swept away by Nature's backhand swipe, a storm surge. It is in this turbulent environment that the wits of the wildfowler is pitted against the wildest of our wildlife, the silent and deadly creep of an incoming tide, and the rage of the heavens in the depths of winter.

Even though nowadays the wildfowler is perforce regulated by clubs and associations, it is still a solitary sport and the image of the 'lone 'fowler' is still strong. A deep love of the wilderness and its wildlife is part and parcel of the commitment, and nobody can be regarded as a true devotee of the sport without being a skilled ornithologist in the truest sense of the word.

In all my wildfowling experience, I have never seen a bird-spotting 'twitcher' on the saltmarsh at dawn or dusk. I once arrived on the sea wall in the afternoon to see a phalanx of anorak-clad people gazing through tripod-mounted telescopes aimed at the marsh. Apparently a rare bird had been reported on the internet and they were determined to tick it off their list. My cheerful greeting as I passed among them was either ignored or answered in a perfunctory manner, perhaps because in these 'bird-lover's' eyes I was carrying a sleeved gun so I was one of those ruthless killers that shoot birds.

Before leaving the bank I noticed that in their hurry to get their sighting, farm gates had been broken down, arable crops had been driven over, and all considerations of private property had been ignored. I dropped down onto the marsh and looked back. There was the most wonderful flight of curlew, enormous numbers coming back to the saltmarsh from their inland feeding grounds, large flocks of golden plover wheeled overhead, and redshank flitted back and forth along the creek at the foot of the bank, hurling their customary abuse at the crowds of humans that had disturbed their activities. All this was ignored by the telescope-hugging fraternity. So which of us, I asked myself, are the true naturalists and 'bird lovers'? I settled into my hide as the sun reached the horizon, the offshore wind had picked up and I hoped for a good wigeon flight later on as the twilight deepened. I looked back at the sea wall, it was deserted.

Some philosopher once claimed that one could never appreciate true happiness without at least once experiencing the depths of despair. I can apply this to wildfowling. There are many lonely vigils on the saltmarsh in harsh winter weather and in poor light, when I have neither sight nor sound of geese or wigeon, when I have the long return to the car, tired, wet, chilled to the core, and very miserable. Just occasionally, the exhilaration of a wonderful winter dawn on a rising tide, a flight of wildfowl scything through the wind, and a feathered bundle or two in our bag makes it all so very worthwhile. Nowadays, I am never alone as Pam is my constant wildfowling companion and shares all the miseries and joys of the sport.

The whistle and rush of a wigeon pack in the darkness, the distant wail of a lapwing in the dead of night, the mournful call of the curlew echoing across a misty marsh dawn, and most of all the far carrying clamour of pink-footed geese as the skeins fill the sky with magic and wild mystery. These are the irresistible sounds of Britain's wildest and loneliest places. These sounds and images are so indelibly imprinted on my mind, so easily conjured up in my imagination, that the words forming the title of this book, spoken in jest by Graham Wall, can only have a temporary relevance after a blank and miserable few hours on the marsh.

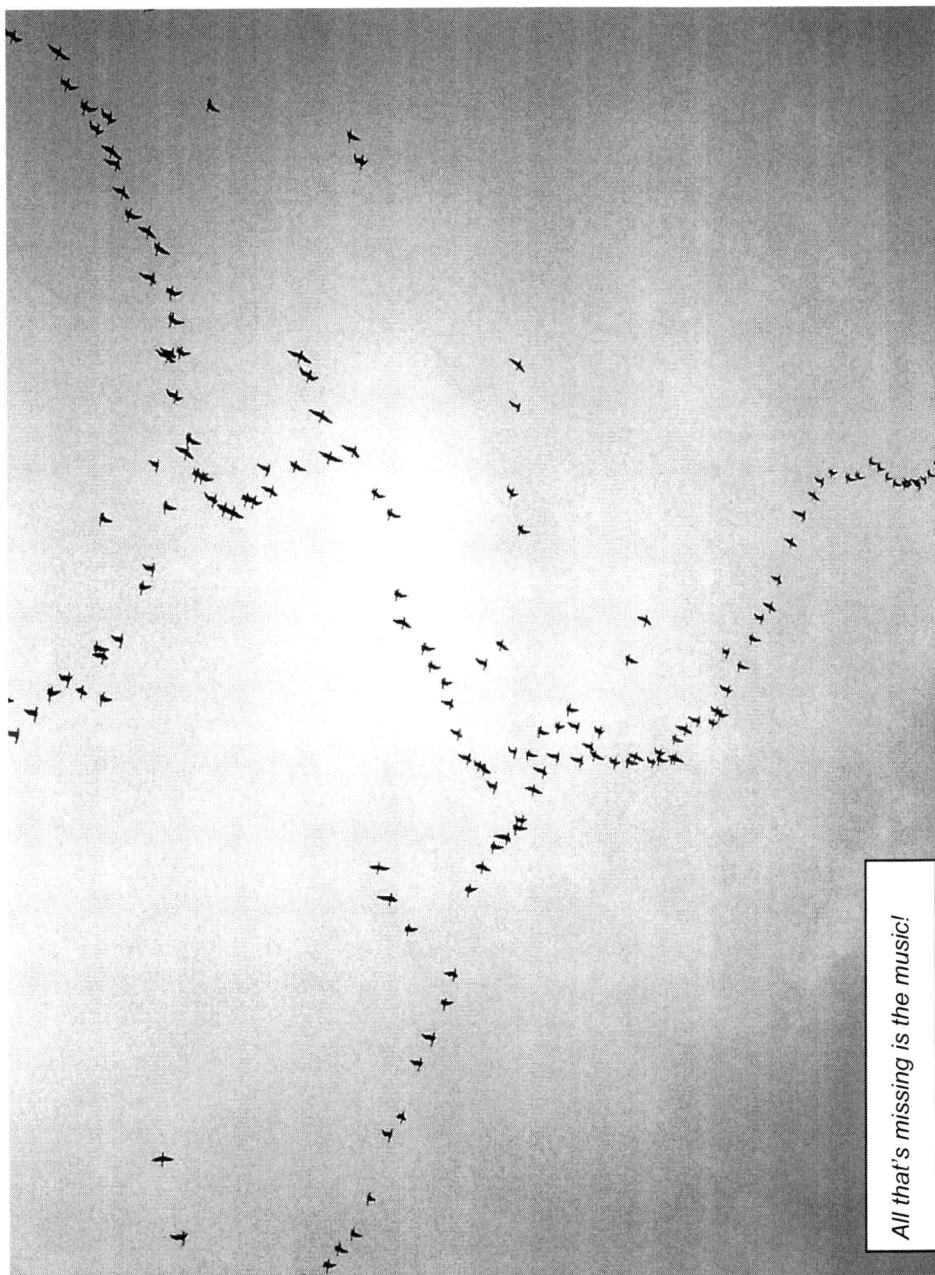

All that's missing is the music!